M000317172

A-10C: Operations Procedures

U.S. Air Force

The BiblioGov Project is an effort to expand awareness of the public documents and records of the U.S. Government via print publications. In broadening the public understanding of government and its work, an enlightened democracy can grow and prosper. Ranging from historic Congressional Bills to the most recent Budget of the United States Government, the BiblioGov Project spans a wealth of government information. These works are now made available through an environmentally friendly, print-on-demand basis, using only what is necessary to meet the required demands of an interested public. We invite you to learn of the records of the U.S. Government, heightening the knowledge and debate that can lead from such publications.

Included are the following Collections:

Budget of The United States Government
Presidential Documents
United States Code
Education Reports from ERIC
GAO Reports
History of Bills
House Rules and Manual
Public and Private Laws

Code of Federal Regulations
Congressional Documents
Economic Indicators
Federal Register
Government Manuals
House Journal
Privacy act Issuances
Statutes at Large

BY ORDER OF THE
SECRETARY OF THE AIR FORCE

AIR FORCE INSTRUCTION 11-2A-10C,
VOLUME 3

22 MARCH 2012

Flying Operations

A-10C -- OPERATIONS PROCEDURES

COMPLIANCE WITH THIS PUBLICATION IS MANDATORY

ACCESSIBILITY: Publications and forms are available for downloading or ordering on the e-Publishing website at **www.e-publishing.af.mil**

RELEASABILITY: There are no releasability restrictions on this publication.

OPR: ACC/A3TO

Supersedes: AFI11-2A-OA-10V3,
               11 February 2002

Certified by: AF/A3O-A
(Col James W. Crowhurst)
Pages: 88

This volume implements AFPD 11-2, *Aircraft Rules and Procedures*; AFPD 11-4, *Aviation Service*; and AFI 11-202V3, *General Flight Rules*. It provides guidance and procedures for the safe and successful operation of A-10 aircraft. This publication applies to all units assigned to or gained by major commands (MAJCOM) and AF direct reporting units (DRU) and applies to commanders, operations supervisors and aircrews assigned or attached to all flying activities of these MAJCOMs and DRUs. When an exception exists to the requirements of a paragraph, the exception is indicated in a parenthetical within the paragraph, or by using subparagraphs directed at specific units. Prior to publication MAJCOMs/DRUs/FOAs are to forward proposed MAJCOM/DRU/FOA-level supplements to this volume to AFFSA/A3OF, through ACC/A3TO, for approval IAW AFPD 11-2, paragraph **4.2**, Records Disposition. Copies of MAJCOM/DRU/FOA-level supplements, after approved and published, will be provided by the issuing MAJCOM/DRU/FOA to AFFSA/A3OF, ACC/A3TO, and the user MAJCOM and ANG offices of primary responsibility. Field units below MAJCOM/DRU/FOA level will forward copies of their supplements to this publication to their parent MAJCOM/DRU/FOA office of primary responsibility for post publication review. Keep supplements current by complying with AFI 33-360, *Publications and Forms Management*. See paragraph **1.5** of this volume for guidance on submitting comments and suggesting improvements to this publication. This publication requires the collection and or maintenance of information protected by the Privacy Act (PA) of 1974. The authorities to collect and or maintain the records prescribed in this publication are Title 10, United States Code, Chapter 857 and Executive Order 9397, Numbering System for Federal Accounts Relating to Individual Persons, November 22, 1943. Forms affected by the PA have an appropriate PA statement. System of records notice F011 AF XO A, *Aviation Resource Management System (ARMS)* (December 26, 2002, 67 FR 78777) applies. Paperwork Reduction Act of 1974 as amended in 1996 affects this instruction. Ensure that all records created as a result of processes prescribed in this publication are maintained in accordance with Air Force Manual (AFMAN) 33-363, *Management of Records*, and disposed of in accordance with the Air Force Records Disposition Schedule (RDS) maintained in the Air Force Records Information Management System (AFRIMS) located at "**https://www.my.af.mil/afrims/afrims/afrims/rims.cfm**." Recommendations for improvements to this volume will be submitted on AF Form 847, *Recommendation for Change of Publication,* through channels, to the parent MAJCOM Stan/Eval. Parent MAJCOM Stan/Eval will forward approved recommendations to lead command OPR (ACC/A3T, 205 Dodd Blvd, Suite 101, Langley AFB VA 23665-2789). AF/A3/5 is the approval authority for changes to this instruction.

SUMMARY OF CHANGES

This revision incorporates Interim Change (IC) 2002-1. This change deletes references to the OA-10, A-10A, and A-10A with SMFCD; adds references to the A-10C; replaces GFAC with JTAC and AFAC with FAC(A); and updates AFTTP 3-1.A-10, *Tactical Employment*, and AFTTP 3-3.A-10, *Combat Aircraft Fundamentals*, references. It delegates waiver authority for those forces presented to a COMAFFOR (paragraph **1.3**); adds clarification for approval of squadron standards (paragraph **2.2.2**); adds fuel conservation considerations (paragraph **2.2.3**); standardizes flight briefing requirements (paragraphs **2.6**); changes minimum external lighting requirements to reflect FAR Part 91.209 (paragraph **3.2.5**); adds considerations for rolling takeoffs (paragraphs **3.6.2** and **3.6.6**); standardizes general formation responsibilities and deconfliction (paragraphs **3.9** and **3.9.1**); modifies guidance for G-awareness exercise (paragraph **3.13.2**); adds guidance for ops checks (paragraph **3.14**); adds TGP minimum altitudes (paragraph **3.17.17**); adds NVG takeoff and landing requirements (paragraph **3.20.3.2**); standardizes Trail Procedures and adds Trail Recovery procedures (paragraph **4.3**); adds requirement for working slat and stall warning systems for ACBT (paragraph **5.1.4**); adds prohibition of maintaining stall warning AOA during ACBT (paragraph **5.2.2**); clarifies guidance for simulated air-to-air attack switchology (paragraphs **5.3** and **5.4**); modifies target ID considerations to incorporate ACC SII guidance and A-10C capabilities (paragraph **6.4.2**); clarifies guidance for simulated air-to-ground attack switchology (paragraph **6.6**); updates web location of the authorized list of LCP and LEP devices (paragraph **6.9**); standardizes general roles and responsibilities in special subjects briefing guide (paragraph **A3.1**); adds Chemical, Biological, Nuclear and High-Yield Explosive (CBRNE) information from rescinded AFMAN 10-2602, *Nuclear, Biological, Chemical, and Conventional (NBCC) Defense Operations and Standards*, (**Attachment 16**).

Chapter 1

INTRODUCTION

1.1. Responsibilities. This volume, in conjunction with other governing directives, prescribes procedures for operating A-10C aircraft under most circumstances. It is not a substitute for sound judgment or common sense. Procedures not specifically address may be accomplished if they enhance safe and effective mission accomplishment.

1.2. Waivers. Unless another approval authority is cited, waiver authority for this volume is MAJCOM/A3, or COMAFFOR for those pilots and assets under a COMAFFOR's oversight. Waivers are issued for a maximum of one year from the effective date. COMAFFOR will notify ACC/A3 and home station MAJCOM/A3 of waivers within 72 hours of approval.

1.3. Deviations. In the case of an urgent requirement or aircraft emergency the pilot in command (PIC) will take appropriate action(s) to safely recover the aircraft. If time permits specific approval of the MAJCOM/A3 or COMAFFOR will be obtained for one time deviations from these procedures.

1.4. Processing Changes.

1.4.1. Submit recommended changes and questions about this publication through MAJCOM channels to the Office of Primary Responsibility (OPR) per AFI 11-215, *USAF Flight Manuals Program (FMP)* using AF Form 847.

1.4.2. The submitting MAJCOM will forward information copies of AF Forms 847 to all other MAJCOMS that use this publication. Using MAJCOMs will forward comments on AF Forms 847 to the OPR.

1.4.3. OPR will:

1.4.3.1. Coordinate all changes to the basic instruction with affected MAJCOM/A3s.

1.4.3.2. Forward change recommendations to AFFSA for staffing and AF/A3 approval.

1.5. References. This instruction, in conjunction with the documents listed in the subparagraphs below, are the primary references for A-10C operating procedures. Training units may develop phase manuals from the procedures contained in these documents. Phase manuals may expand these basic procedures; however, in no case will they be less restrictive, nor will they change the procedures in these documents.

1.5.1. T.O. 1A-10C-1, *A-10C Flight Manual*

1.5.2. T.O. 1A-10C-34-1-1, *A-10C Non-Nuclear Weapons Delivery Manual*

1.5.3. Air Force Tactics, Techniques, and Procedures (AFTTP) 3-1.A-10, *Tactical Employment-- A-10.*

1.5.4. AFTTP 3-3.A-10, *Combat Aircraft Fundamentals-- A-10.*

1.5.5. AFI 11-214, *Aircrew, Weapons Director, and Terminal Attack Controller Procedures for Air Operation.*

Chapter 2

MISSION PLANNING

2.1. Responsibilities. The responsibility for mission planning is shared jointly by all flight members as well as the ops and intel functions in the unit.

2.2. General Procedures. Accomplish sufficient flight planning to ensure safe mission accomplishment to include fuel requirements, map preparation and takeoff/landing data.

2.2.1. In addition, consult the following for mission planning:

2.2.1.1. AFI 11-202V3

2.2.1.2. AFI 11-214.

2.2.2. Standards. The Squadron Commander (SQ/CC) is the approval authority for squadron standards. Ops Group Commander (OG/CC) may publish and approve group or wing standards. Ops Group Stan/Eval (OGV) will review all standards for compliance with AFI 11-series guidance.

2.2.3. Fuel Conservation. Aviation fuel is a limited commodity and precious resource. Consider fuel efficiency throughout all phases of mission planning and execution. Design flight plans and routing for optimal fuel use. Consider in-flight procedures such as climb/descent profiles and power settings for efficient fuel usage.

2.3. Map/Chart Preparation:

2.3.1. Local Area Maps. A local area map is not required if pilot aids include jettison areas, divert information, controlled bail-out areas and provide sufficient detail of the local area to remain within assigned training areas.

2.3.2. VFR navigation above 3000 ft AGL. Flight Information Publication (FLIP) enroute charts may be used instead of maps on navigational flights within areas adequately covered by these charts.

2.3.3. Low Altitude Map Requirements. During low altitude segments of a flight (below 3,000 feet AGL), each pilot must operate with at least one of the following maps available for all segments (either TAD or paper copy).

2.3.3.1. Current sectional aeronautical chart.

2.3.3.2. A current and CHUM updated (either ECHUM or manual) NGA map of the low altitude route/operating area. The map will be of such scale and quality that terrain features and required items displayed to allow navigation and safe mission accomplishment. The following items must be specifically displayed by the actual map or by other means (overlay, drawfile, handwritten, etc.): Airports/heliports, Special Use Airspace (SUAs) boundaries, ICAO class B/C/D boundaries, other airspace boundaries, MTRs, parachute jump and; and other potential high density traffic areas (flight activity areas and ultra light/hang glider/glider sites, etc.)

2.3.4. Specifically developed low level route books require the previous items indicated within 5 nm of the route or MTR lateral boundary.

2.3.5. Use of electronic maps does not relieve pilots from their responsibility to thoroughly brief all routes, pertinent obstacles, applicable airfield approach control frequencies in the vicinity of class A/B/C/D airspace, intersection of other Visual Routes (VR)/Instrument Routes (IR) (if applicable), and any other possible areas of conflicts.

2.3.6. Pilots flying outside CONUS will follow gaining MAJCOM, theater or host nation guidance on mission planning. If no gaining MAJCOM, theater or host nation guidance exists, use the best available maps or electronic overlay options to accomplish the requirements of paragraph **2.3.3.2**

2.4. Unit-Developed Checklist/Local Pilot Aids:

2.4.1. Unit developed checklists of flight manual checklists may be used provided they contain, as a minimum, all items (verbatim and in order) listed in the applicable checklist.

2.4.2. Locally developed pilot aids will be produced. As a minimum, include the following:

2.4.2.1. Briefing guides.

2.4.2.2. Local radio channelization and airfield diagrams.

2.4.2.3. Impoundment procedures, emergency action checklists, and No Radio (NORDO)/divert information.

2.4.2.4. Cross-country procedures to include: command and control, engine documentation, Joint Oil Analysis Program (JOAP) samples, servicing, manual reversion ground checks and other information as deemed necessary by individual units (e.g.,stereo flight plans, turnaround procedures, local training areas and bailout/jettison areas).

2.4.2.5. Other information as deemed necessary by the units (i.e. stereo flight plans, local training area diagrams, and local area maps of sufficient detail to provide situational awareness on area boundaries).

2.5. Mission Data Cards. Squadron-generated line-up cards may be used if they contain the necessary information for the type of mission being flown. As a minimum, required items are:

2.5.1. Callsign.

2.5.2. Minimum Takeoff Landing Data (TOLD) requirements on Mission Data Cards are

2.5.2.1. Acceleration check speed,

2.5.2.2. Refusal/maximum abort speed (dry/wet),

2.5.2.3. Takeoff speed/distance, and

2.5.2.4. Normal/heavyweight landing distance (dry/wet).

2.5.3. Joker and Bingo fuels will be annotated.

2.6. Preflight Brief.

2.6.1. All flight members must attend the flight brief unless previously coordinated with unit supervisors.

2.6.2. Anyone not attending the flight brief must receive, as a minimum, a brief on mission events and emergency procedures (EP) prior to step.

2.6.3. Flight leads/instructors are responsible for presenting a logical brief which will promote safe and effective mission accomplishment.

2.6.3.1. Ensure brief start time provides adequate time to discuss required items and accounts for mission complexity. As a minimum, begin briefs at least 1.5 hours before scheduled takeoff. Alert briefs will start in sufficient time to be completed prior to aircrew changeover.

2.6.3.2. Structure the brief to accommodate the capabilities of each flight member.

2.6.3.3. Ensure contracts, roles, and responsibilities of each flight member are established, briefed, and debriefed.

2.6.3.4. Review TOLD and ensure every member of the flight understands it. Place particular emphasis on takeoff abort factors during abnormal situations such as short or wet runway, heavy gross weights, and abort sequence in formation flights.

2.7. Alternate Mission Briefs. Brief an appropriate alternate mission for each flight.

2.7.1. The alternate mission must be less complex than the primary mission (e.g. Basic Fighter Maneuvers as alternate for Air Combat Maneuvers, Basic Surface Attack for Surface Attack Tactics).

2.7.2. If the alternate mission does not parallel the planned mission, brief the specific mission elements that are different.

2.7.3. Mission elements may be modified and briefed airborne as long as flight safety is not compromised. Flight leads will ensure changes are acknowledged by all flight members.

2.7.4. Do not fly unbriefed (either on the ground or in the air) missions or events.

2.8. Briefing Guides.

2.8.1. Reference the attachments to this AFI for basic briefing guide examples.

2.8.2. Subjects may be briefed in any sequence.

2.8.3. Those items published in AFIs, AFTTP or unit standards and understood by all participants may be briefed as standard.

2.9. Multiple Sortie Days.

2.9.1. If all flight members attend an initial or mass flight brief, the flight lead on subsequent flights need brief only those items that have changed from the previous flight(s).

2.9.2. On multiple-go days when aircraft turn times do not allow follow-on mission brief(s) and only the initial flight brief is accomplished for all goes, the following guidance applies:

2.9.2.1. Upgrade missions should be flown on the first sortie but may be flown on the second sortie if the first is non-effective for weather, maintenance, or airspace availability.

2.9.2.2. Subsequent missions will be of equal or less complexity with no additional upgrade training, unless approved by OG/CC.

2.9.2.3. Participants in continuation training (CT) missions may fly their primary or alternate missions in any sequence.

2.10. Postflight Debrief.

2.10.1. All missions will be debriefed.

2.10.2. All flight debriefs will include, at a minimum, the in-flight execution of flight member responsibilities, deconfliction contracts, tactical employment priorities, and task management.

Chapter 3

NORMAL OPERATING PROCEDURES

3.1. Cockpit Preflight. Pilots will take special care when using and storing extra equipment in the cockpit that is not part of the integral cockpit design. Pilots are to ensure the placement of equipment is secured throughout all phases of flight, night or day, to prevent inadvertent contact with crucial cockpit switches. Units will determine if an operational necessity exists for the NVG case strap and remove the strap if it is not needed.

3.1.1. Ground Visual Signals. Normally, pilot and ground crew will communicate by the intercom system during all Starting Engines, Before Taxi and End of Runway (EOR) checks. Use the intercom system to the maximum extent possible anytime maintenance technicians are performing "redballs" on the aircraft. The pilot will not activate any system that could pose any danger to the ground crew prior to receiving proper acknowledgment from ground personnel. When not using ground intercom, visual signals will be in accordance with AFI 11-218, *Aircraft Operation and Movement on the Ground,* and this volume. The crew chief will repeat the given signal when it is safe to operate the system. The following signals augment AFI 11-218:

3.2. Starting Engines and Before Taxiing:

3.2.1. Pilots will be cleared by the crew chief prior to starting the APU, engines or actuating primary or secondary flight controls.

3.2.2. All flights require the bleed air function of the APU.

3.2.3. Aircraft stall warning devices will be fully operational for all flights.

3.2.4. In addition to the requirements of AFI 11-202V3, General Flight Rules, as supplemented and FLIP, the following equipment will be operative if IMC is anticipated at any point in the flight:

3.2.4.1. Tactical air navigation (TACAN).

3.2.4.2. Heading attitude reference system (HARS).

3.2.4.3. Standby attitude indicator.

3.2.5. Minimum required operational exterior lighting for night flying is: Landing and taxi light, both wingtip position lights, 1 out of 2 wingtip strobe anti-collision lights and at least one of the tail lights, either the fuselage tail position (stinger) light or strobe anti-collision light.

3.3. Taxi:

3.3.1. Minimum taxi interval is 150 feet. Spacing may be reduced when holding short of or entering the runway.

3.3.1.1. Minimum taxi interval is 300 feet at night, when carrying live bombs, and when operating on a Runway Conditions Reading (RCR) of less than 12.

3.3.2. Quick Check and Arming. Place hands in view of ground personnel while the quick check inspection, arming/de-arming, and/or hot refueling are in progress.

3.3.3. Do not taxi in front of aircraft being armed/de-armed with forward firing ordnance.

3.3.4. When ice or snow is present, aircraft will not be taxied until all portions of the taxi route and runway have been checked for safe conditions. Units will specify minimum RCR for taxi operations.

3.4. Flight Lineup. Flights will line up appropriately based on weather conditions, runway conditions and runway width. Spacing between separated elements/flights will be a minimum of 500 feet. If performing formation takeoffs, wingmen must maintain wingtip clearance with their element leader. If runway width precludes line up with wingtip clearance between all aircraft in the flight, use 500 feet spacing between elements or delay run-up until the preceding aircraft has released brakes.

3.4.1. Normally place wingman on the upwind side if the crosswind component exceeds 5 knots.

3.5. Lineup Checks. After completing the "Lineup Checks" and prior to takeoff, all flight members will inspect each other for proper configuration and any abnormalities. Wingmen will indicate they are ready for takeoff by a head nod, radio call, or landing/taxi light signal as briefed.

3.6. Takeoff:

3.6.1. Do not attempt a takeoff if the RCR is less than 12 or as specified otherwise by MAJCOM.

3.6.1.1. Per MAJCOM guidance, OG/CC may waive RCR minimum for specified units operating in cold weather locations, but in no case will takeoffs be conducted with an RCR of less than 8.

3.6.2. On training missions, do not takeoff if the computed takeoff roll exceeds 80 percent of the available runway single ship, or 70 percent for a formation or rolling takeoff.

3.6.3. If a VFR takeoff is required for mission accomplishment, the aircraft must be capable of achieving a minimum single-engine climb rate of 150 feet/minute (gear up, failed engine windmilling, flaps up, fuel flows normal, and all jettisonable stores-jettisoned), unless a higher rate of climb is required for unique obstacle clearance requirements. IFR takeoffs will be conducted IAW AFI 11-202V3. Aircraft operating under IFR that are unable to comply with the required minimum climb gradients may be required to reduce fuel and ordnance loads, cart selected stores , or wait for environmental conditions to change. If operational requirements dictate, takeoffs may be made without a positive single-engine climb rate when approved by OG/CC

3.6.4. If operational requirements dictate, intersection takeoffs may be approved by the OG/CC.

3.6.5. Takeoff interval between aircraft/elements will be a minimum of 10 seconds except for chased takeoffs. When accomplishing a join-up on top or when carrying live ordnance, (excluding 30mm, rockets, flares or air-to-air missiles) increase takeoff interval to a minimum of 20 seconds.

3.6.6. For rolling takeoffs, pilots will ensure the aircraft is aligned with the runway centerline prior to engaging anti-skid and advancing throttles. Only accomplish rolling takeoffs on icy runways or unimproved surfaces.

3.7. Formation Takeoff:

3.7.1. Formation takeoffs are restricted to elements of two aircraft.

3.7.2. A qualified flight lead will lead all elements unless an Instructor Pilot (IP), or flight lead qualified squadron supervisor, is in the element.

3.7.2.1. Formation takeoff weather requirements are 300/1nm(1.6km) or Pilot Weather Category (PWC), whichever is higher

3.7.3. Formation takeoffs will not be made when:

3.7.3.1. Runway width is less than 140 feet.

3.7.3.2. Standing water, ice, slush or snow is on the runway.

3.7.3.3. RCR is less than 12.

3.7.3.4. The crosswind or gust component exceeds 15 knots.

3.7.3.5. Computed takeoff roll in excess of 70 percent of available runway length.

3.7.3.6. Loaded with live munitions (excluding 30mm, rockets, flares or air-to-air missiles).

3.7.3.7. Ferrying aircraft from contractor/ALC facilities.

3.7.4. Configure aircraft so as not to exceed an asymmetrical load moment of 12,000 foot-pounds.

3.7.4.1. When asymmetrical loading is expected to create a noticeable rolling moment, the runway line-up will be such that both aircraft will not roll toward each other on liftoff.

3.7.4.2. Formation takeoffs with aircraft not similarly configured can be made if the asymmetry in configurations include one of the following

3.7.4.2.1. A rack plus practice bombs,

3.7.4.2.2. A rocket/flare dispenser,

3.7.4.2.3. A TGM 65, or

3.7.4.2.4. An air-to-air missile or an ECM pod (except ALQ-184).

3.7.5. Differences in aircraft gross weight will not exceed 2,000 pounds. Takeoff data will be computed for the heavier aircraft.

3.7.6. Formation Takeoff Procedures. Refer to AFTTP 3-3.A-10.

3.7.6.1. On the flight lead's signal, set the core RPM at 90 percent or as briefed by the flight lead and check the engine instruments. In hot weather, 90 percent core RPM may not give predicted takeoff fan speed. In this instance, set one percent below predicted takeoff fan speed.

3.7.6.2. Smoothly add power after brake release. If lead needs to reduce power for the wingman on takeoff, he will not reduce throttles beyond 3 percent below predicted takeoff fan speed or min/abort fan speed, whichever is higher.

3.7.6.3. Maintain wingtip clearance throughout takeoff roll. If the wingman overruns the leader, the leader will direct the wingman to assume the lead, at which time the wingman will push up to MAX power, maintain his side of the runway, and make his own takeoff. The original leader will then be responsible for in-flight separation and directing appropriate measures to regain flight integrity or initiate lost wingman procedures. The original wingman will fly the briefed departure until instructed otherwise by the flight leader.

3.7.6.4. Retract the gear after the flight leader observes the wingman to be safely airborne.

3.8. Join-up/Rejoin:

3.8.1. Day weather criteria for a join-up underneath a ceiling is 1,500 feet and 3 miles.

3.8.1.1. Flight leaders will maintain 200 KIAS until join-up is accomplished unless briefed otherwise.

3.8.1.2. If accomplishing a turning join-up, the flight leader will normally not exceed 30 degrees of bank.

3.8.1.3. Flight members will join in sequence. For a straight ahead rejoin, the number two aircraft will join on the left wing and the element will join on the right wing unless otherwise briefed. For a turning rejoin, the number two aircraft will rejoin on the inside of the turn and the element to the outside. If mission or flight requirements dictate, the flight leader will specifically call and state the desired formation positions.

3.8.1.4. For further join-up procedures, see paragraph **3.10** and **Chapter 4**.

3.9. Formation, General: Flight leads/IPs are responsible for ensuring contracts, roles and responsibilities of each flight member are established, briefed, executed and debriefed. If any flight member cannot fulfill their basic responsibilities, contracts, or other assigned tasks, they will immediately communicate that information to the flight/element lead. IP/flight leads will task element leads/wingmen based on their ability to fulfill basic responsibilities and other assigned tasks. For additional formation considerations, reference AFTTP 3-3.A-10 and AFTTP 3-1.A-10. Situational Awareness Data Link (SADL) will not be used as the sole or primary source of deconfliction.

3.9.1. The flight lead will supervise formations. The flight lead retains responsibility for the flight regardless of which physical position he flies. Wingmen should have the situational awareness to be prepared to fly the number one position if, in the judgment of the flight lead, such action is warranted. The term element lead may be used to designate the number three aircraft in a flight of four—this, in itself, does not imply flight lead authority.

3.9.2. Do not perform rolling maneuvers during join-up/rejoins to non-tactical formation.

3.9.3. Do not perform rolling maneuvers to maintain or regain position below 5,000 feet AGL or in airspace where aerobatics are prohibited.

3.9.4. Airborne visual signals will be in accordance with AFI 11-205, *Aircraft Cockpit and Formation Flight Signals*. For four ship flights, initiate configuration changes by radio call, when practical. When formation position changes are directed by radio, all wingmen will acknowledge prior to initiating the change. A radio call is mandatory when directing position changes at night or under instrument conditions.

3.9.5. Flight leaders will not break up formations until each pilot has a positive fix from which to navigate (visual, Air Traffic Control (ATC), EGI, or TACAN).

3.9.6. In IMC, maximum flight size in close formation is four aircraft except when flying in formation with a tanker.

3.9.7. Changing Leads. Refer to AFTTP 3-3.A-10.

3.9.7.1. The minimum altitude for changing leads within a formation/element in day VMC is 500 feet AGL over land or 1,000 feet AGL over water, except for emergencies (for night see paragraph **3.19.4**; for IMC, see paragraph **4.6**).

3.9.7.2. Prior to initiating the lead change, the leader will ensure that the wingman assuming the lead is in a position to safely initiate the lead change.

3.9.8. Transitioning to instrument meteorological conditions (IMC):

3.9.8.1. When flying in visual meteorological conditions (VMC) with a high potential for IMC, flight leads should place their formations in close, route, or trail. Avoid using wedge or fighting wing to skirt marginal weather.

3.9.8.2. If loss of sight inadvertently occurs due to weather while in a VMC formation, the following applies:

3.9.8.2.1. Maintain VMC if feasible; transmit "call sign, blind, altitude, and heading."

3.9.8.2.2. If unable to maintain VMC, immediately transition to instruments, recover to level or climbing flight, and execute the appropriate lost wingman procedures. The flight lead will ensure altitude separation between other aircraft in the flight until separate Instrument Flight Rules (IFR) clearances can be obtained.

3.9.8.2.3. If unable to maintain VMC while low level, execute low level abort procedure while transitioning to instruments. See paragraph **3.17.16**

3.9.9. Wingmen may practice low altitude tactical navigation (LATN) provided the route was thoroughly briefed and the flight lead maintains navigation situational awareness. Wingmen may lead portions of a mission provided an instructor pilot (IP) or flight lead qualified squadron supervisor is in the same element.

3.9.10. Close Formation.   Except for lazy-eight or chandelle-type maneuvers, close formation aerobatics will not be flown.

3.10. Tactical Formations:

3.10.1. Tactical Maneuvering.   Refer to AFTTP 3-1 AFTTP 3-3.A-10 and MAJCOM directives. The following rules apply for flight path deconfliction during tactical maneuvering:

3.10.1.1. Flight/element leads will consider wingman/element position and ability to safely perform a maneuver before directing it.

3.10.1.2. Wingmen/elements maneuver relative to the flight lead/lead element and maintain sight. Trailing aircraft/elements will be responsible for deconfliction with lead aircraft/elements. SADL may be used to augment situational awareness when flying tactical formations.

3.10.1.3. Wingmen/elements go high and/or outside of the lead/lead element for deconfliction when required.

3.10.1.4. For rejoins from tactical formation, the wingman will join to the side of the formation occupied at the time the rejoin is directed. If in trail, join to the left side. In all cases, the trailing element will join to the side opposite the number two, unless otherwise directed.

3.10.2. Lost Visual Contact. The following procedures apply when one or more flight members/elements lose visual contact within the formation.

3.10.2.1. If any flight member/element calls "blind," then the other flight member/element will immediately confirm a "visual" with an informative/directive radio call.

3.10.2.2. If the other flight member/element is also blind, then the flight lead will take action to ensure altitude separation based on the cockpit altimeter or sector deconfliction off a known point. Use a minimum of 500 feet altitude separation when directed to deconflict by altitude. Avoid climbs/descents through the deconfliction altitude. Low Altitude Safety and Targeting Enhancement (LASTE) HUD altimeter readings should not be used as the primary altitude reference for deconfliction due to the potential of significantly different altimeter readings if not operating in NAV mode. Once deconfliction is assured, pilots may use SADL to assist in regaining visual.

3.10.2.3. If there is no timely acknowledgment of the original "blind" call, then the flight member/element initiating the call will maneuver away from the last known position of the other flight member/element and alter altitude.

3.10.2.4. If visual contact is still not regained, the flight leader will take additional positive action to ensure flight path deconfliction within both the flight and the scenario to include a "Terminate/Knock-It-Off," as appropriate. Consider scenario restrictions such as sanctuary altitudes and/or adversary blocks.

3.10.2.5. Aircraft will maintain altitude or sector separation until regaining visual and will continue to maintain this separation until regaining mutual support.

3.10.3. Two-Ship. Normally, the wingman is responsible for flight path deconfliction. The flight lead has primary responsibility for deconfliction when:

3.10.3.1. Tactical maneuvering places the leader in a position likely to cause the wingman to lose sight of the leader or forces the wingman's primary attention away from the leader (e.g., wingman becomes the defensive or engaged fighter).

3.10.3.2. The wingman calls "padlocked."

3.10.3.3. The wingman calls "blind."

3.10.3.4. Primary deconfliction responsibility transfers back to the wingman once the wingman acknowledges "visual" on lead.

3.10.4. **Three/Four-Ship (or Greater).** When flights of more than two aircraft are in tactical formation:

3.10.4.1. Formation visual signals performed by a flight/element leader pertain only to the associated element unless specified otherwise by the flight leader.

3.10.4.2. Trailing aircraft/element(s) will maintain a sufficient distance back so that primary emphasis during formation maneuvering/turns is on low altitude awareness and deconfliction within elements, not on deconfliction between elements.

3.11. Chase Formation. Refer to AFTTP 3-3.A-10.

3.11.1. Restrictions:

3.11.1.1. Any pilot may fly safety chase for aircraft under emergency or impending emergency conditions. Qualified pilots (pilots who have successfully completed an Instrument/Qualification evaluation including Initial Qualification Training (IQT)/ Mission Qualification Training (MQT) pilots) may chase as a safety observer for aircraft performing simulated instrument flight, hung ordnance recovery, or simulated single engine patterns. All other chase events will be flown by flight examiners, IPs, Upgrading IPs supervised by an IP, or flight lead qualified squadron supervisors designated by the Squadron Director of Operations (SQ/DO).

3.11.1.2. During takeoff, the chase aircraft will maintain a minimum of nose-to-tail and wing tip clearance. All formation takeoff restrictions apply except chased takeoffs may be accomplished if computed takeoff roll is in excess of 70 percent of available runway length and/or the crosswind or gust component exceeds 15 knots. Brief specific abort procedures.

3.11.1.3. In flight, the chase aircraft will maneuver as necessary, but must maintain nose-tail separation. The chase will not stack below the lead aircraft below 1,000 feet AGL.

3.11.1.3.1. When moving into or out of close formation from chase, the chase pilot will make a radio call indicating intentions. The call indicating a move to close formation will be acknowledged.

3.11.1.4. In the traffic pattern, the chase aircraft may maneuver as necessary to observe performance.

3.11.1.5. Confidence Maneuver Chase. The chase pilot will fly a pattern well clear of the maneuvering aircraft's flight path. The chase aircraft will not perform the confidence maneuver simultaneously.

3.11.1.6. When chasing live ordnance missions, the chase pilot is responsible for ensuring safe escape criteria is met.

3.11.1.7. A safety observer in a chase aircraft will maneuver in an approximate 30 to 60 degree cone with nose/tail clearance to 1,000 feet, to provide assistance and effective clearing.

3.12. Show Formation. Refer to AFI 11-209, *Air Force Participation in Aerial Events*, and applicable MAJCOM directives for guidance. Specifically, brief these formations and fly them IAW applicable directives and AFTTP 3-3.A-10. Wing/group commander approval is required.

3.13. Maneuvering Parameters:

3.13.1. Use T.O. 1A-10A-1, T.O. 1A-10C-1, MAJCOM operating procedures, AFTTP 3-1.A-10, and AFTTP 3-3.A-10 to define and describe the performance of weapons deliveries, confidence maneuvers, aerobatics, Air Combat Training (ACBT), or advanced handling maneuvers.

3.13.2. G-awareness exercise will be accomplished IAW AFI 11-214, gaining MAJCOM, theater and host nation guidance. Any mission that plans or is likely to maneuver in excess of five Gs will accomplish a G-awareness exercise IAW AFTTP 3-3.A-10. Missions planned at five Gs or less do not require this exercise. G-awareness exercise will be filmed and in Hot Mic.

3.13.2.1. Unless performing a syllabus-required event (e.g. chase of a G-awareness exercise), flight members will maintain a minimum of 6,000 feet separation between aircraft during the execution of all G-awareness exercises. On board systems (e.g., air-to-air TACAN, data link) should be used to establish and maintain separation prior to maneuver execution. During maneuver execution use visual lookout and briefed formation contracts as primary means of ensuring aircraft deconfliction. If required, use on board systems to enhance situational awareness during the maneuver.

3.13.2.2. G-awareness exercise is not required at night. If a G-awareness exercise is performed, pilots must have NVGs and enough visual cues to perform this maneuver. Flight leads will ensure spacing between elements is sufficient to maintain deconfliction between all flight members. Consideration should be given to splitting the elements for separate G awareness exercises.

3.13.2.3. Flight/element leads will ensure the airspace intended for conducting the G-awareness exercise is free from potential traffic conflicts. Use air traffic control (ATC) services to the maximum extent practical to make sure the airspace is clear. Conduct the G-awareness exercise in the following airspace with preference to the order as listed:

3.13.2.3.1. Special use airspace (e.g., Restricted/Warning areas, ATCAAs, MOAs and MAJCOM approved large scale exercise/special missions areas).

3.13.2.3.2. Above 10,000 feet MSL outside of special use airspace.

3.13.2.3.3. Inside the confines of Military Training Routes.

3.13.2.3.4. Below 10,000 feet MSL outside of Special Use Airspace.

3.13.3. Minimum Altitudes:

3.13.3.1. Confidence Maneuvers—Entry will be made at a minimum of 10,000 feet AGL.

3.13.3.2. Do not perform aerobatics below 5,000 feet AGL.

3.13.4. Vortices/Jetwash. Avoid flight through wing tip vortices/jetwash. If unavoidable, unload the aircraft immediately to approximately 1 G.

3.13.5. Use of Flaps. Do not use flaps as an in-flight maneuvering aid in the conduct of aerial combat maneuvers. The Maneuver (MVR) position may be used in the landing pattern, when loitering, when escorting another aircraft, etc.

3.14. Ops Checks:

3.14.1. Accomplish sufficient ops checks to ensure safe mission accomplishment. For formation flights, the flight lead will initiate ops checks by radio call or visual signal. Wingmen will respond by radio call or visual signal.

3.14.2. Ops checks are required:

3.14.2.1. During climb or at level-off after takeoff.

3.14.2.2. When internal wing tanks or external fuel tanks (if carried) are empty. When internal wing tanks are dry, ops checks will include "wings dry." When carrying external tanks, ops checks will include "tanks feeding" or "tanks dry" as appropriate. Once the external tank(s) and/or internal wing tanks are confirmed and called dry, omit this call from subsequent ops checks.

3.14.2.3. After completing air refueling.

3.14.2.4. Prior to each air to air engagement (Basic Fighter Maneuvers (BFM), Air Combat Maneuvering (ACM), and (Dissimilar) ((D)ACBT).

3.14.2.5. Prior to commencing air-to-surface operations, at least once during air-to-surface operations, and after terminating air-to-surface operations.

3.14.3. Do not use data linked fuel status as the primary reference for fuel checks. Data link may not display accurate fuel remaining and does not verify wing tank balance or status of forward/aft main tank balance problems.

3.15. Radio Procedures. Use the complete flight call sign anytime any flight member initiates a radio transmission. In all other cases, an acknowledgment by flight position is sufficient. Use "Knock It Off" (KIO) or "Terminate" procedures to direct aircraft to stop engagements, scenarios and tactical maneuvering IAW AFI 11-214. All flight members will acknowledge by repeating the call.

3.15.1. Brief the use of backup/alternate radios within a flight and monitor closely. Use of these radios as an "intra-flight intercom" or for administrative information that should be held for debriefing is inappropriate and constitutes poor radio discipline.

3.15.2. The flight/mission leader will initiate all frequency changes with either the term "PUSH" or the term "GO." If "PUSH" is used flight members will change to the new frequency without an acknowledgement. If "GO" is used each flight member will acknowledge, in turn, prior to any flight member switching frequencies. Flight/mission leader will initiate a radio check on the new frequency which will be acknowledged, in turn, by all flight members. **EXCEPTION:** During prebriefed radio silent training or limited comm operations, channel changes will be as briefed.

3.15.3. Individual flight members, in turn, will acknowledge radio checks that do not require the transmission of specific data. Acknowledgment by the individual flight member indicates the initiation or completion of the appropriate check.

3.15.4. In addition to the standard radio procedures outlined in AFI 11-202V3; Specific Mission Guides; and FLIP publications; the following radio transmissions are required:

3.15.4.1. All flight members will acknowledge understanding the initial ATC clearance. Acknowledge subsequent ATC instructions when directed by the flight lead or anytime during trail departures.

3.15.4.2. Gear down calls will be IAW AFI 11-202V3 and AFI 11-217V1, *Instrument Flight Procedures*. Wingman or chase aircraft are not required to make an individual gear down call during a formation of chased approach.

3.15.5. When requiring simultaneous action by other flight members, the voice command will be followed by the word of execution "NOW."

3.15.6. Brevity code and other terminology will be IAW AFI 11-214, AFTTP 3-1, and AFJPAM 10-228.

3.16. Airborne Communications Jamming Procedures. Refer to AFI 11-214.

3.17. General Low Altitude Procedures:

3.17.1. Fly low-level formation positions/tactics using AFTTP 3-1.A-10 and AFTTP 3-3.A-10 as guides.

3.17.2. Fly line abreast formation at or above 300 feet AGL. When flying in formation below 300 feet AGL the wingman will be directed to a wedge, trail, or combat trail formation position. Training in the 300 to 100 feet AGL altitude block will be in short segments consistent with real-world risks and realistic tactical considerations.

3.17.3. For air-to-surface range operations, minimum altitudes will be determined by area/range restrictions, AFI 11-214 restrictions or delivery restrictions, whichever is greater. "Show of Force" is not a weapons delivery maneuver and will be flown IAW the pilot's minimum altitude, area/range restrictions or theater SPINs, whichever is higher.

3.17.4. At altitudes below 1,000 feet AGL, wingmen will not fly at a lower AGL altitude than lead.

3.17.4.1. Some formations will have flight leads LASDT certified lower than their wingmen. The flight lead that flies lower than other formation members will, prior to descending to their block, confirm their wingmen's low altitude warning is set to their minimum altitude.

3.17.5. Flights operating in the low altitude environment will climb to a prebriefed safe altitude (minimum 1,000 feet AGL) when a Knock-It-Off is called.

3.17.6. Navigate using a combination of pilotage, dead reckoning (DR) and Embedded GPS/INS (EGI) information. DR will be the primary means of navigation.

3.17.7. If unable to visually acquire or ensure lateral separation from known vertical obstructions, which are a factor to the planned route or flight, flight leads will direct a climb to ensure vertical separation 2 NM prior to the obstacle.

3.17.8. When crossing high or hilly terrain, do not exceed 120 degrees of bank. Limit zero or negative G crossings to upright bunting maneuvers that are within the zero/negative G limitations for the aircraft and external stores.

3.17.9. Minimum flight planning airspeed for low altitude flight/navigation is 240 KIAS. Minimum airspeed during low altitude flight/navigation is 200 KIAS.

3.17.10. For aircraft equipped with an operable radar altimeter, the system will be on and set at either the briefed minimum altitude or the command-directed low level altitude, whichever is higher.

3.17.11. The unit commander, IAW AFI 11-2A-10, Volume 1, *A-10—Aircrew Training,* as supplemented, will determine and certify a pilot's minimum altitude. Pilots participating in approved step-down training programs will comply with the requirements and restrictions of that program. Unless higher altitudes are specified by national rules, route restrictions, or training syllabus, the following minimum altitudes apply to low level training:

3.17.11.1. 500 feet AGL for:

3.17.11.1.1. Formal Training Unit (FTU) students and instructors when conducting training IAW an applicable syllabus.

3.17.11.1.2. Pilots who have not entered step-down training or are not certified for flight at lower altitudes.

3.17.11.1.3. Overwater flight if duration is more than 1 minute or if out of sight of land or if there is an indefinite horizon.

3.17.12. Minimum Safe Altitude (MSA) will provide a clearance of 1,000 feet above the highest obstacle/terrain feature (rounded to the next highest 100 feet) within 5 NM of the planned course, route boundaries, or operating area (e.g. military operating area (MOA), low fly area, restricted area, etc.). Pilots may compute an MSA for each leg/segment of the intended route of flight or for a specific target.

3.17.12.1. For night (non-NVG) or IMC operations, the minimum altitude is MSA.

3.17.13. When external tanks are installed, do not fly missions requiring tactical maneuvering at low altitudes. EXCEPTION: Low altitude tactical maneuvering within Dash 1 limits is authorized with an installed centerline Sergeant Fletcher external tank.

3.17.14. During all low altitude operations, the immediate reaction to task saturation, diverted attention, or an emergency, is to climb.

3.17.15. Weather minimums for visual low-level training will be 1,500 feet and 3 miles, or as directed by Host Nation for any route or area or as specified in FLIP for Military Training Routes (i.e., 3,000/5 for VR routes), whichever is higher.

3.17.16. Low-Level Route/Area Abort (RAA) Procedures. Compute and brief a low-level route abort altitude (RAA). The RAA will provide a clearance of 1,000 feet above the highest obstacle/terrain feature (rounded to the next highest 100 feet) within 5 NM of the entire planned course, route boundaries or operating area (e.g., MOA, low fly area, restricted area, etc.). Minimum airspeed for the route abort is 160 KIAS. Maximum pitch angle is 30 degrees nose high.

3.17.16.1. VMC Route/Area Abort Procedures:

3.17.16.1.1. Maintain safe separation from the terrain.

3.17.16.1.2. Comply with VFR altitude restrictions and squawk appropriate (IFF/SIF) modes and codes.

3.17.16.1.3. Maintain VMC at all times. If unable, follow IMC procedures outlined below.

3.17.16.1.4. Attempt contact with controlling agency, if required.

3.17.16.2. IMC Route/Area Abort Procedures:

3.17.16.2.1. During low level flight, every safe effort will be made to avoid entering IMC. If IMC is encountered, pilots will transmit Call sign, knock-it-off and route abort.

3.17.16.2.2. Immediately climb to, or above the briefed RAA. Transition to instruments if entering IMC.

3.17.16.2.3. A route abort is an emergency procedure and pilot judgment is paramount. Flight leads will ensure safe separation while complying with local/host nation procedures. If deviation from local/host nation procedures is necessary to avoid a collision, the flight lead will direct the appropriate action.

3.17.16.2.4. Maintain preplanned ground track. Execute appropriate lost wingman procedures if necessary. The flight/element leader is responsible for ensuring heading and/or altitude deconfliction during an IMC route abort procedure. Ensure deconfliction is based on the same altimeter setting.

3.17.16.2.5. Use the current altimeter setting until changed by the flight lead and squawk emergency or in compliance with host nation procedures.

3.17.16.2.6. If required to deviate from normal route/area procedures, or if the RAA is higher than the vertical limits of the route/area, squawk (IFF/SIF) emergency.

3.17.17. Targeting Pod (TGP) Minimum Altitudes. These minimums apply to heads down operations while manipulating the TGP such as searching for targets through the MFCD. Minimum altitude for this type of TGP employment is 5,000 feet AGL, except when doing self-mark HAS with a base altitude above 5,000 feet AGL and recovery altitude IAW AFI 11-214 minimums. Pilots who have completed the TGP LASDT upgrade may use the following minimum altitudes:

3.17.17.1. 1,000 feet AGL during day

3.17.17.2. 2,000 feet AGL for night/high illumination

3.17.17.3. 2,000 feet AGL or MSA, whichever is higher, for night/low illumination

3.17.18. Use of TGP LSS/LST capability below altitudes prescribed in paragraph **3.17.17** above is limited to HOTAS actions required to initiate and display LSS/LST symbology in the HUD or Helmet Mounted Cueing System (HMCS).

3.17.18.1. Intent of low altitude LSS/LST use is for pilots to keep their eyes outside the cockpit for target area SA and acquisition. These systems should be used to provide pilots a "pure heads up and outside" capability without requiring heads down time during employment.

3.18. Air Refueling:

3.18.1. Pilots undergoing initial/recurrency training in air refueling will not refuel with a student boom operator (does not apply to KC-10).

3.18.2. Pilots will inform boom operator when refueling from particular tanker type (e.g. KC-10, KC-135, or other) for the first time.

3.18.3. Pilots will not attempt a night hook-up if slipway lights are inoperative unless refueling is necessary to safely complete the mission.

3.19. Night Operational Procedures:

3.19.1. Night Ground Operations. Taxi spacing will be a minimum of 300 feet and the aircraft will taxi on the taxiway centerline. Normally, use the taxi light during all night taxiing. (**EXCEPTION:** When the light might interfere with the vision of the pilot of an aircraft landing or taking off, the taxiing aircraft will come to a stop if the area cannot be visually cleared without the taxi light.)

3.19.2. Night Takeoff. For formation takeoffs, flight/element leaders will turn the anti-collision strobes OFF and position lights BRIGHT (DIM as desired) STEADY when reaching the run-up position on the runway. The flight/element lead may direct wingmen to turn or leave the strobes OFF anytime the lights cause distraction. All aircraft will turn formation lights ON. During a night formation takeoff, call brake release and configuration changes over the radio. Following takeoff, each aircraft/element will climb on runway heading to 1,000 feet AGL and accelerate to 200 KIAS before initiating turns, except where departure instructions/local procedures/obstructions specifically preclude compliance.

3.19.3. Night Join-up. Weather criteria for night join-up underneath a ceiling is 1,500 feet and 3 miles. Accomplish join-up/rejoin at or above 1,000 feet AGL. During the rejoin, wingmen will cross check their altimeter to ensure they remain at least 1,000 feet AGL. After join up, the anti-collision strobes will be OFF and position lights will be BRIGHT (DIM if necessary) STEADY for all except the last aircraft. The last aircraft will keep the anti-collision strobe ON and position lights BRIGHT STEADY unless otherwise directed by the flight lead.

3.19.4. Night Formation Procedures.

3.19.4.1. -(Non-NVG equipped.) When in positions other than fingertip or route, maintain aircraft spacing primarily by instruments (radial/DME,or Air-to-Air TACAN) and/or timing, with visual reference and SADL secondary. If unable to ensure aircraft spacing, then establish altitude separation (minimum of 1,000 feet). At all times, pilots will cross-check instruments to ensure ground clearance.

3.19.4.2. Change of lead or wing positions must be accomplished at or above 1,500 feet AGL, unless established on radar downwind. Lead and position changes will be called over the radio and should be initiated from stabilized, wings-level attitude.

3.19.5. Night Breakup. Prior to a night formation breakup, the flight leader will confirm position and transmit altitude, airspeed, attitude, altimeter setting and heading. Wingmen will acknowledge to confirm good navigational aids.

3.20. Night Vision Goggles (NVG) Procedures: Pilots must not become overconfident in the capabilities of NVGs. Many things can cause a pilot to lose outside visual references, to include entering the weather (intentionally or inadvertently), NVG battery failure, flight into smoke or dust, flight into a shadowed area, sudden illumination or an incompatible light source inside or outside of the cockpit, or sudden distractions due to an aircraft malfunction, etc. Pilots must ensure primary and secondary flight instruments are sufficiently illuminated to allow for immediate transition to instruments if experiencing spatial disorientation or if outside visual references are lost.

3.20.1. Published Guidance. USAF/MAJCOM guidance (including AFI 11-202V3 and AFI 11-214) outlines NVG procedures. Additionally:

3.20.1.1. NVGs will only be worn in flight by NVG qualified pilots or by upgrading pilots with a qualified NVG IP in the flight.

3.20.1.2. NVG operations below 5,000 feet AGL require an operational Ground Collision Avoidance System (GCAS).

3.20.1.3. All flight members will make a radio call when going "goggles on" or "goggles off" and only one flight member will don/doff goggles at a time.

3.20.2. NVGs must be preflight tested and adjusted for the individual pilot in a unit eyelane or equivalent tester prior to NVG operations

3.20.3. Takeoff and Landing.

3.20.3.1. Non-NVG Takeoff and Landing qualified pilots will not wear NVGs during takeoff or landing. Do not don NVGs until at least 2,000 feet AGL or MSA, whichever is higher, in climbing or level flight. Remove NVGs at least 5 minutes prior to landing.

3.20.3.2. NVG takeoff and landing qualified pilots may wear NVGs for takeoff and landing. NVG takeoffs and landings at a blacked-out aerodrome configured with AMP-3 (covert) lighting will be flown in aircraft equipped with an infrared (IR) cover installed on the taxi light. NVG operations at airfields with normal (overt) lighting do not require the IR cover installed on the taxi light. Do not accomplish NVG approaches to an airfield with a combination of covert and overt runway lighting unless that specific configuration is tested and approved. Weather minimums for certified pilots to perform NVG takeoff and landing operations are 1500/3. Weather minimums during upgrade training for certification are 3000/5.

3.20.4. Illumination Levels:

3.20.4.1. High Illumination is defined as a minimum of 2.2 millilux illumination derived from natural or artificial sources. This roughly equates to a 20% moon disk at an elevation of 30 degrees or higher. If weather or other conditions reduce actual in-flight illumination below 2.2 millilux, low illumination procedures will be followed.

3.20.4.2. Low Illumination is defined as less than 2.2 millilux.

3.20.4.3. Even when illumination levels are forecast, weather or other conditions may cause actual illumination levels to be higher or lower than expected. In flight, pilots must estimate whether actual in-flight illumination levels are High or Low, and determine if the existing conditions provide sufficient NVG performance to accomplish the planned mission and/or events. Pilots will comply with High or Low illumination procedures/restrictions contained here and in AFI 11-214.

3.20.5. NVG Minimum Altitudes. Minimum altitudes for NVG operations are based on illumination levels, in-flight visibility, and the pilot's NVG qualification.

3.20.5.1. The minimum altitude for all NVG upgrade sorties, familiarization sorties/events, sorties flown under low illumination levels, or sorties flown when in-flight visibility is less than 5 miles is the MSA, as defined in paragraph **3.17.12**, or IAW AFI 11-214, whichever is higher.

3.20.5.2. The minimum altitude for all other NVG sorties flown under high illumination levels and with at least 5 miles in-flight visibility is IAW AFI 11-214 and MAJCOM supplements to AFI 11-214.

3.20.6. Tanker Rejoin. NVGs may be worn for night tanker rejoins, but will be raised to the up and stowed position or removed no later than the precontact position and remain off through the actual contact and AAR. Goggles may be worn pre and post AAR in the observation position and in route position flying off the tanker.

3.20.7. Close Formation. Wingmen wearing NVGs will fly no closer than route formation.

3.20.8. Weather Restriction. MAJCOM established night weather restrictions apply. Pilots must be ready to transition to instruments and execute appropriate lost wingman or route abort procedures in the event they inadvertently enter the weather. Under certain IMC or marginal VFR conditions, NVGs may allow pilots to maintain visual references with relation to the ground, the horizon, other aircraft, etc. However, while wearing NVGs pilots must still comply with published VFR cloud clearance and visibility minimums, have an IFR clearance prior to entering IMC, and follow all IFR procedures while in IMC.

3.20.9. Weapons Delivery:

3.20.9.1. Range weather restrictions and minimum altitudes during weapons delivery passes are IAW AFI 11-214. Minimum altitudes during night surface attack operations are IAW AFI 11-214 restrictions, the pilot's NVG qualification minimum altitude, and the minimum altitude allowed by the actual illumination level, whichever is higher.

3.20.9.2. On Class A ranges, NVG qualified pilots, with the concurrence of the Range Control Officer (RCO), are allowed to choose external aircraft lighting settings that maximize training, minimize interference with NVGs, and still allow the RCO to safely monitor the aircraft. Depending on the lighting conditions and RCO equipment, this could involve normal, reduced, covert or blacked-out lighting IAW AFI 11-214.

3.20.9.3. NVG qualified pilots may conduct normal, reduced, covert or blacked-out lighting weapons deliveries IAW AFI 11-214 on ranges which do not require RCO control. When working with a Joint Terminal Attack Controller (JTAC) or Forward Air Controller (Airborne) (FAC(A)), pilots should choose external lighting settings that safely facilitate final control.

3.20.9.4. During all range sorties for upgrading NVG pilots (basic NVG upgrade), covert or blacked-out lighting weapons deliveries may only be conducted dry.

3.21. Fuel Requirements:

3.21.1. Joker Fuel. A pre-briefed fuel needed to terminate an event and proceed with the remainder of the mission.

3.21.2. Bingo Fuel. A pre-briefed fuel state that allows the aircraft to return to the base of intended landing or alternate, if required, using preplanned recovery parameters and arriving with normal recovery fuel as defined below.

3.21.3. Normal Recovery Fuel. The fuel on initial or at the final approach fix (FAF) at the base of intended landing or alternate. Establish fuel quantity locally or 1,500 pounds, whichever is higher.

3.21.4. Minimum Fuel. Declared whenever it becomes apparent that an aircraft will enter initial or start an instrument final approach at the base of intended landing, or alternate if required, with 1,200 pounds or less (or as established locally), or when either the Left or Right Main Fuel Low light illuminates, whichever occurs first.

3.21.5. Emergency Fuel. Declared whenever it becomes apparent that an aircraft will enter initial or start an instrument final approach at the base of intended landing, or alternate if required, with 800 pounds or less, or 400 pounds in either the left or right main system, whichever occurs first.

3.22. Approaches and Landings:

3.22.1. Minimum pattern and touchdown spacing. Refer to AFI11-202V3 ACCSUP, Chapter 5. Use touchdown spacing requirements listed for dissimilar fighter aircraft when wind conditions increase the likelihood of encountering wake turbulence.

3.22.2. The desired touchdown point for a VFR approach is 500 feet past the runway threshold, or the glidepath interception point for a precision approach. When local procedures or unique runway surface conditions require landing beyond a given point on the runway, adjust the desired touchdown point accordingly.

3.22.3. Landing Restrictions:

3.22.3.1. When the computed landing roll exceeds 80 percent of the available runway, land at an alternate if possible.

3.22.3.2. Minimum landing RCR is 12. Per MAJCOM guidance, OG/CC may waive the minimum RCR, but in no case will landing be attempted with an RCR below 8.

3.22.3.3. Do not land over any raised web barrier (e.g., MA-1A, 61QS11).

3.22.4. Normally all aircraft will land in the center of the runway and clear to the turnoff side of the runway when speed/conditions permit, unless local conditions dictate otherwise.

3.23. Overhead Traffic Patterns:

3.23.1. Altitude and airspeed will be IAW T.O. 1A-10C-1 or as directed locally.

3.23.2. Overhead patterns may be flown with unexpended practice ordnance to include heavyweight inerts, night illumination flares, 30 mm, unexpended live air-to-air and forward firing ordnance. Overhead patterns may be performed at deployed locations with unexpended live ordnance if required by local force protection arrival procedures.

3.23.3. Initiate the break over the touchdown point or as directed.

3.23.4. Execute the break individually in a level 180 degree turn to the downwind leg at minimum intervals of 5 seconds (except IP/SEFE chase or when in tactical formation).

3.23.5. Aircraft will be wings level on final at approximately 300 feet AGL and 1 mile from the planned touchdown point.

3.24. Tactical Overhead Traffic Patterns:

3.24.1. Tactical entry to the overhead traffic pattern is permitted if the following conditions are met:

3.24.1.1. Use published overhead pattern altitude and airspeed.

3.24.1.2. Locally develop and coordinate with appropriate air traffic control agencies specific procedures.

3.24.1.3. Four aircraft are the maximum permitted. Aircraft/elements more than 6,000 feet in trail are considered a separate flight.

3.24.1.4. Normally position wingmen opposite the direction of the break.

3.24.1.5. Regardless of the formation flown, no aircraft should be offset from the runway in the direction of the break; the intent is to avoid requiring a tighter than normal turn to arrive on normal downwind.

3.24.1.6. Fly normal downwind and base position.

3.25. Low Approaches:

3.25.1. Observe the following minimum altitudes:

3.25.1.1. Normal single ship slow approaches—so that touchdown does not occur.

3.25.1.2. IP/SEFE chase position—50 feet AGL.

3.25.1.3. Formation low approaches (and non-IP/SEFE chase)--100 feet AGL.

3.25.1.4. Chase aircraft during an emergency—300 feet AGL unless safety or circumstances dictate otherwise.

3.25.2. Go-Arounds: During go-around, remain 500 feet below VFR overhead traffic pattern altitude until crossing the departure end of the runway unless local procedures, missed approach/climb-out procedures, or controller instructions dictate otherwise.

3.26. Closed Traffic Patterns. Initiate the pattern at the departure end of the runway unless directed/cleared otherwise by local procedures or the controlling agency. Minimum airspeed during a closed pattern, prior to configuring, is 150 KIAS. When in formation, a sequential closed may be flown with ATC concurrence, at an interval to ensure proper spacing.

3.27. Formation Approaches and Landings:

3.27.1. General:

3.27.1.1. Normally accomplish formation landings from a precision approach. If not, accomplish landing utilizing a published instrument approach or a VFR straight-in approach using the VASI if available. In all cases, the rate of descent should be similar to a normal precision approach.

3.27.1.2. A flight leader will lead continuation training formation landings. Upgrading flight leads require an IP or SQ/DO designated flight lead qualified supervisor in the element.

3.27.1.3. When only one aircraft is landing from a formation approach, normally the lead will execute a low approach and the wingman will land. In this event, the wingman will break off for landing as briefed, as cleared by the leader, or in the case of poor positioning, accomplish a low approach.

3.27.1.4. Do not perform practice formation approaches above 40,000 pounds gross weight.

3.27.2. Formation Landing Restrictions. Aircraft configuration will be IAW paragraph **3.7.4** Formation landings are prohibited:

3.27.2.1. When the cross wind or gust component exceeds 15 knots.

3.27.2.2. When the runway is reported wet; or ice, slush, or snow are on the runway.

3.27.2.3. If runway width is less than 140 feet.

3.27.2.4. When landing with hung ordnance or unexpended live ordnance (excluding live air-to-air missiles, rockets, night illumination flares and 30mm ammunition).

3.27.2.5. If the weather is less than 500 feet and 1 1/2 miles or a flight member's weather category, whichever is higher.

3.27.3. Lead Procedures. Refer to AFTTP 3-3.A-10.

3.27.3.1. Establish an approach speed consistent with the heavier aircraft. Approach speeds may be adjusted higher than standard approach speeds, depending on turbulence, runway length, runway condition, etc.

3.27.3.2. Position the wingman on the upwind side if the cross wind component exceeds 5 knots.

3.27.3.3. Plan to land near the center of your half of the runway to ensure enough runway is available for the wingman.

3.27.4. Wingman Procedures. Refer to AFTTP 3-3.A-10.

3.27.4.1. Maintain a minimum of 10 feet lateral wingtip spacing.

3.27.4.2. Cross-check the runway to ensure proper runway alignment.

3.27.4.3. Execute a climbout/missed approach if sufficient runway/aircraft clearance is not available.

3.27.5. Roll-out Procedures. Refer to AFTTP 3-3.A-10.

3.27.5.1. If the wingman overruns the leader, accept the overrun and maintain aircraft control on the appropriate side of the runway. Do not attempt to reposition behind the leader. The most important consideration is wing tip clearance.

3.28. Chaff/Flare/Smoky Devil Procedures. AFI 11-214 contains basic procedures for employment of Chaff/Flare/Smoky Devils.

3.28.1. Do not arm chaff/flare systems unless in an approved area with the intent to dispense chaff and/or flares.

3.28.2. Minimum employment altitude for Smoky Devils is 500 feet AGL.

Chapter 4

INSTRUMENT PROCEDURES

4.1. Approach Category:

4.1.1. The A-10 is Approach Category D. Accomplish missed approach in accordance with the flight manual procedures. Missed approach airspeed is 200 to 220 KIAS.

4.1.2. Approach category C minima may be used to an emergency/divert airfield where no Category D minima is published, provided:

4.1.2.1. A straight-in approach is flown.

4.1.2.2. The aircraft is flown at a computed final approach speed of 140 KIAS or less.

4.1.2.3. Missed approach airspeed is 200 to 210 KIAS.

4.1.3. Missed approach airspeeds are based on 260 KTAS or less for Category D approaches and 240 KTAS or less for Category C approaches. At high pressure altitudes and temperatures, these true airspeeds may not be compatible with published missed approach airspeeds and the approach should not be flown.

4.1.4. A-10s are approved to use INS for enroute Area Navigation (RNAV) for a period not to exceed 1 ½ hours between INS updates. An update is defined as establishing/validating a positive position using visual references, GPS, or TACAN. A-10s are approved to use EGI for point-to-point navigation only. Do not fly (GPS or RNAV) on Q and T-routes, or terminal procedures (approaches and STARs) without MAJCOM approval.

4.2. Takeoff and Join-up:

4.2.1. The flight lead will notify the appropriate ATC agency when a VMC join-up is not possible due to weather conditions or operational requirements. Coordinate for an appropriate altitude block and trail formation. Formation trail departures will comply with instructions for a non-standard formation flight as defined in FLIP. Flight lead should request IFF squawks for wingmen in trail.

4.3. Trail Procedures.

4.3.1. General. Do not sacrifice basic instrument flying when performing secondary tasks during trail departures in IMC. Strictly adhere to the briefed airspeeds, power settings, altitudes, headings, and turn points. If task saturation occurs, cease attempts to maintain trail, immediately concentrate on flying the instrument procedure, and notify the flight lead. Flight lead will notify ATC.

4.3.2. Trail Departure:

4.3.2.1. Use a minimum of 20 seconds takeoff spacing.

4.3.2.2. Each aircraft/element will accelerate in MAX power to 200 KIAS. Climb speed will be 200 KIAS and power setting will be 800 degrees ITT unless specifically briefed otherwise.

4.3.2.3. Each aircraft/element will climb on takeoff heading to 1,000 feet AGL and accelerate to 200 KIAS before initiating any turns, except when departure instructions specifically preclude compliance.

4.3.2.4. Each aircraft/element will call passing each 2,000 foot altitude increment (or as briefed) with altitude and heading passing if in a turn until join-up or level off. In addition, each aircraft/element will call initiating any altitude or heading change. Acknowledgments are not required; however, it is imperative that preceding aircraft/elements monitor the radio transmissions and progress of the succeeding aircraft/elements and adhere to the departure route.

4.3.2.5. Each aircraft/element will maintain the briefed trail takeoff spacing using all available aircraft systems and navigational aids to monitor positions.

4.3.2.6. Each aircraft/element will maintain at least 1,000 feet vertical separation from the preceding aircraft/element during the climb, at level off, and in cruise until visual contact is established, except in instances where departure instructions specifically preclude compliance. If unable to comply with MEA or ATC is unable to accommodate 1,000 foot blocks, vertical separation may be reduced to 500 feet.

4.3.3. Trail Recovery:

4.3.3.1. Trail recovery procedures must be coordinated/approved through the responsible ATC facilities and addressed in the unit supplement to this volume. Trail recoveries will only be accomplished at home stations/deployed locations where procedures have been established and briefed. As a minimum, procedures will address each recovery profile, missed approach, climbout, lost contact, lost communications and desired/maximum spacing requirements.

4.3.3.2. Trail recoveries are limited to a maximum of four aircraft.

4.3.3.3. Trail recoveries are authorized when weather at the base of intended landing is at/above the highest pilot weather category in the flight or approach minimums, whichever is higher.

4.3.3.4. Trail recoveries will not terminate in simultaneous radar or circling approaches. If these are required, flights will break up IAW paragraph **4.4** and obtain separate IFR clearances prior to the final segment of the approach.

4.3.3.5. Flight leads will brief spacing, configuration, and airspeeds. Minimum spacing between aircraft is 6,000 feet and will be maintained using all available aircraft systems and navigational aids.

4.3.3.6. Prior to taking spacing, flight leads will coordinate with ATC and ensure that all wingmen have operative navigational aids IAW paragraph **4.4** The formation will squawk as directed by ATC.

4.3.3.7. ATC instructions to the lead aircraft will be for the entire flight. ATC will provide radar flight following for the entire formation.

4.3.3.8. All turns are limited to a maximum of 30 degrees of bank.

4.3.3.9. Once established on a segment of a published approach, each aircraft will comply with all published altitudes and restrictions while maintaining trail separation.

4.3.3.10. Unless local procedures establish defined reference points for airspeed/configuration changes, the flight lead will direct changes by radio. When directed, all aircraft in the formation will comply simultaneously.

4.3.3.11. If SA is lost or separation/deconfliction cannot be guaranteed during recovery, the flight lead will establish altitude deconfliction and coordinate a separate IFR clearance with ATC. If this occurs after established on a segment of a published approach, the pilot will execute a missed approach or climbout as directed by ATC.

4.4. Formation Breakup/Spacing Procedures. Formation breakup should not be accomplished in IMC; however, if unavoidable, accomplish the breakup in straight and level flight. Prior to a weather breakup, the flight leader will transmit attitude, airspeed, altitude, altimeter setting, and heading. All wingmen acknowledge the transmission and confirm good navigational aids.

4.5. Formation Penetration:

4.5.1. Formation penetrations are restricted to two aircraft when the weather at the base of intended landing is less than overhead traffic pattern minimums.

4.5.2. If flying a formation landing, the wingman should be positioned on the appropriate wing prior to weather penetration.

4.6. Formation Lead Changes in IMC. In IMC, formation flights will not change lead/wing positions below 1,500 feet AGL or instrument downwind altitude, whichever is lower.

4.7. Use of the HUD. The HUD is not certified as a primary flight instrument. It may be used as an additional instrument reference in night/IMC conditions; however, do not use it as the sole instrument reference in these conditions. In addition, do not use the HUD to recover from an unusual attitude or when executing lost wingman procedures except when no other reference is available.

Chapter 5

AIR-TO-AIR WEAPONS EMPLOYMENT

5.1. General:

5.1.1. AFI 11-214 contains air-to-air procedures to include operations with live ordnance (air-to-air missiles) applicable to all aircraft. The procedures contained in this chapter specify additional procedures or restrictions that are applicable to A-10C operations.

5.1.2. This chapter applies to all missions where the intent is to conduct maneuvers used to defeat aerial attacks or to employ ordnance against airborne fixed wing aircraft or helicopters. Fixed wing air-to-air training should emphasize visual acquisition of threats, maneuvering to negate any attack, mutual support, and forcing the attacker to disengage. Anti-helicopter air-to-air training should emphasize visual search techniques, maneuvers to negate helicopter attacks, aspect and range determination, and weapons selection and employment to kill the threat.

5.1.3. During high-aspect BFM training, a dedicated defender and offender must be clearly identified for each engagement. The offender will have some kind of advantage (power, G available, lead turn advantage at the merge, energy state at start of engagement).

5.1.4. Prior to conducting ACBT, pilots will maneuver the aircraft to confirm proper operation of slats, peak performance (steady tone) and stall warning (chopped tone). If any component of the stall warning system does not appear to be functioning properly, do not conduct ACBT maneuvering.

5.1.5. Do not conduct Air-to-Air training with hung ordnance.

5.2. Maneuvering Limits:

5.2.1. The minimum airspeed during ACBT is 120 KIAS.

5.2.2. During ACBT maneuvering, pilots will not maintain an angle of attack (AOA) that triggers the chopped stall warning tone. If the chopped tone is activated, relax back pressure immediately to return to an AOA that deactivates the chopped tone.

5.2.3. The minimum maneuvering airspeed during low altitude air-to-air training is 240 KIAS for both defensive and offensive maneuvering.

5.2.4. Negative G guns jinks are prohibited.

5.2.5. Night Air-to-Air weapons events will not be accomplished without specific MAJCOM approval.

5.3. Simulated Gun/AIM-9 Employment.

5.3.1. If the gun is PINNED or UNPINNED, simulated air-to-air weapons employment using the gun trigger or AIM-9 pickle button are allowed when the following conditions are met:

5.3.1.1. No live or heavyweight inert ordnance aboard the aircraft (30MM, BDU-33, and 2.75 rockets are authorized).

5.3.1.2. No hung ordnance.

5.3.1.3. Master Arm switch is in TRAIN.

5.3.1.4. GUN/PAC Arm switch is in SAFE.

5.3.1.5. Flight lead verbally confirms training mode (TRN in the HUD or TRAIN on the MFCD) and GUN/PAC Arm switch SAFE and acknowledged throughout the flight.

5.3.1.6. Cold trigger and pickle check is accomplished and acknowledged throughout the flight.

Chapter 6

AIR-TO-SURFACE WEAPONS EMPLOYMENT

6.1. General. References-- AFTTP 3-1.A-10, AFTTP 3-3.A-10, T.O. 1A-10-34-1-1, T.O. 1A-10-34-1-2, and Fighter Weapons School (FWS) Instructional Texts are primary references for fighter weapons employment theory, planning, techniques and analysis. AFI 11-2A-10V1 contains qualification and scoring criteria. AFI 11-214 contains operating and training procedures. Range sorties with planned BDU-33 deliveries from a TER-9 will be scheduled in elements of two aircraft to the maximum extent possible to allow a Battle Damage Check. This does not preclude scheduling single ship FAC(A) sorties.

6.2. Weather Minimums. Refer to AFI 11-214. Weather ceiling will be no lower than 1,500 ft AGL.

6.3. Battle Damage/Bomb Checks. If circumstances permit, flight leads will direct a battle damage/bomb check prior to or during RTB. This check is mandatory following the expenditure of live ordnance (including all types of 30mm ammunition). Observe established deconfliction responsibilities and position change procedures. Formation spacing will be no closer than normal fingertip. Bomb checks will not be conducted at night.

6.4. Training Rules:

6.4.1. Refer to AFI 11-214. If airspeed decreases below 210 KIAS in a pop-up attack, abort the maneuver. Base this airspeed on typical training weights and configurations. At heavy gross weight, adjust abort airspeed upward to provide sufficient G and turning room to recover from an adverse flight condition.

6.4.2. Pilots must positively identify the target and deconflict ordnance footprints from friendly force positions prior to weapons release. Use all available means in order to acquire the target visually, acquire the target through a Targeting Pod (TGP) or by confirming target location through valid on-board/off-board cues. These cues include target talk-on description, marking rounds, LSS/LST, TGP, HUD symbology, IR pointers or other NVG compatible marking devices. For Inertially Aided Munition (IAM) deliveries using Bomb on Coordinate (BOC), target coordinate read back to the JTAC/FAC(A) must be off the DSMS page.

6.4.2.1. LSS/LST or Pave Penny procedures.

6.4.2.1.1. LSS/LST employment utilizes the concepts of a safety and optimum attack zones.

6.4.2.1.2. Reference JP 3-09.1 for laser safety and optimal attack zones.

6.4.2.1.3. LSS/LST will not be used as a sole source for target identification. In some situations, laser spots shift from the designated target to the laser source while operating in the optimal attack zone—precluding total reliance on the laser spot.

6.4.2.1.4. Attack heading will avoid the target-to-laser designator safety zone to preclude false target indications.

6.4.3. FTU/MQT Pilots:

6.4.3.1. Will not change targets once roll-in to final is initiated except during two-target strafe.

6.4.3.2. Will not perform element pop-ups. This does not preclude IP chase or tactical formation ingress to the target.

6.4.4. Local operational procedures/directives will specify night spacing techniques and order of night weapons deliveries commensurate with aircraft performance, flight manual restrictions and peculiarities of local range geography and target sets. Procedures should ensure performance of the most demanding events after the pilot is acclimated to night weapons deliveries.

6.5. Live Ordnance Procedures:

6.5.1. Refer to AFI 11-214.

6.5.2. When Ground Controllers are operating on Class B/C ranges, the following procedures apply:

6.5.2.1. All pilots will be familiar with applicable range weapons delivery procedures, appropriate targets and weapons footprints.

6.5.2.2. Ground personnel locations will be briefed and acknowledged by all pilots.

6.5.2.3. Pilots will not expend ordnance if any doubt exists as to the ground personnel or intended target locations.

6.6. Simulated Air-to-Surface Weapons Employment:

6.6.1. A simulated attack is defined as an attack in which the pilot presses the weapons release (pickle) button and/or pulls the gun trigger with the intention of conducting a dry pass.

6.6.2. If the gun is PINNED or UNPINNED, simulated attacks against off-range targets are permitted using the gun trigger and pickle button when the following conditions are met:

6.6.2.1. No live or heavyweight inert ordnance aboard the aircraft (30MM, BDU-33, and 2.75 rockets are authorized).

6.6.2.2. No hung ordnance.

6.6.2.3. Established in a MOA or Restricted/Warning area.

6.6.2.4. Master Arm switch is in TRAIN.

6.6.2.5. GUN/PAC Arm switch is in SAFE.

6.6.2.6. Flight lead verbally confirms training mode (TRN in the HUD or TRAIN on the MFCD) and GUN/PAC Arm switch SAFE and acknowledged throughout the flight.

6.6.2.7. Cold trigger and pickle check is accomplished, acknowledged, and confirmed by visual inspection throughout the flight.

6.7. Joint Air Attack Team (JAAT):

6.7.1. References. Reference AFTTP 3-1, JP 3-09.3, and JFire MTTP for additional Tactics, Techniques, and Procedures.

6.7.2. Aircraft/Helicopter Separation. Ensure separation through one or both of the following methods:

6.7.2.1. Altitude blocks with at least 100 feet separation between the top of the helicopter block and the bottom of the A-10 block.

6.7.2.2. Routes, sectors, or timing procedures that ensure deconfliction.

6.7.3. Training Rules. Normal air-to-surface training rules apply, to include calling Knock-It-Off if situational awareness of helicopter positions is lost.

6.7.4. Radio Frequencies. All participants must monitor one common frequency.

6.8. Search and Rescue Training:

6.8.1. AFTTP 3-1 is the primary reference for wartime SAR procedures, techniques and planning. For peacetime SAR considerations, see paragraph **7.12** of this volume.

6.9. Laser Command Pointer (LCP) and Laser Eye Protection (LEP) Procedures: The list of authorized LCP and LEP is located on the ACC/A3TV SharePoint site **https://acc.eim.acc.af.mil/org/A3/A3T/A3TV/CoP/Laser%20Command%20Pointers%20Help%20and%20Guidance/Forms/AllItems.aspx**

6.9.1. Train personnel using MAJCOM approved academics and conduct vision testing IAW the ACC approved hazard minimization plan.

6.9.2. LEP will be utilized IAW AFI 11-214.

6.9.3. LCPs will be utilized IAW AFI 11-214.

6.9.4. LCPs can be used in all warning, restricted, and military operating areas.

Chapter 7

ABNORMAL OPERATING PROCEDURES

7.1. General. This chapter contains procedures to follow when other than normal operations occur. They do not, however, replace or supersede procedures contained in the flight manual or the use of sound judgment.

7.1.1. Accept no aircraft for flight with a known malfunction which would compromise the safe conduct of the flight until completing appropriate corrective actions.

7.1.2. Do not taxi aircraft with malfunctions that affect the nosewheel steering or brake systems.

7.1.3. After isolating and/or correcting a malfunctioning system, do not use that system again unless its use in a degraded mode is essential for recovery. Do not conduct in-flight trouble-shooting after completing flight manual emergency procedures.

7.1.4. When a fuel imbalance is greater than T.O. 1A-10C-1 limits, terminate tactical maneuvering and investigate. If the fuel imbalance was caused by a slow feeding tank that can be corrected, vice a fuel system failure, the mission may continue IAW T.O. 1A-10C-1 guidance. Terminate the mission if fuel imbalance cannot be corrected. Instruments, medium altitude navigation, deployment missions, and level weapons deliveries are authorized profiles to reduce gross weight.

7.2. Ground Aborts:

7.2.1. When a flight member aborts prior to takeoff, the flight leader will normally realign (or align as briefed) flight positions to maintain a numerical call sign sequence. Flight leaders will advise the appropriate agencies of such changes.

7.2.2. A flight of two or more aircraft with only one designated flight lead in the formation must either sympathetically abort or proceed on a pre-briefed single-ship mission should the flight lead abort.

7.2.3. Pilots who do not takeoff with the flight may join the flight at a briefed rendezvous point prior to a tactical event, or may fly a briefed alternate single-ship mission. FTU students may also follow this procedure if allowed by the appropriate syllabus, and approved by the squadron commander or operations officer. If accomplishing a join-up on an air-to-ground range, terminate all events until the joining aircraft has achieved proper spacing.

7.3. Takeoff Aborts:

7.3.1. Prior to flight, every member of the flight will review and understand takeoff and landing data. Place particular emphasis on takeoff and abort factors during abnormal situations such as short/wet runway, heavy gross weights, and abort sequence in formation flights.

7.3.2. If an abort occurs during takeoff roll, clear to the appropriate side of the runway as expeditiously as possible based on position within the element. If this is not feasible because of aircraft control issues, clear straight ahead and consider directing a flight abort for subsequent flight members. As soon as possible, give call sign and state intentions.

Following aircraft will alter takeoff roll to ensure clearance or will abort takeoff if unable to maintain adequate clearance.

7.3.3. Anytime an aircraft experiences a high speed abort and hot brakes are suspected:

7.3.3.1. Declare a ground emergency.

7.3.3.2. Taxi the aircraft to the designated hot brake area and perform hot brake procedures.

7.4. Air Aborts:

7.4.1. If an abort occurs after takeoff, all aircraft will maintain their original numerical call sign when communicating with agencies outside of the flight. Flight Leads may renumber members for ease of communication within the flight.

7.4.2. The pilot of an aborting aircraft will advise the flight leader of the conditions necessitating the abort, intentions and assistance required.

7.4.3. If the flight leader aborts, the designated deputy leader will assume command of the flight.

7.4.4. Escort aborting aircraft with an emergency condition to the field of intended landing. When other than an emergency condition exists, the flight leader will determine if the aborting aircraft requires an escort.

7.4.5. Abort the mission, regardless of apparent damage or subsequent normal operation, for any of the following:

7.4.5.1. Birdstrike/foreign object damage.

7.4.5.2. Over-G. The aircraft will land as soon as practical out of a straight-in approach.

7.4.5.3. Flight control system anomalies. Declare an emergency, even if the malfunction appears corrected.

7.4.5.4. Engine flameout/stagnation or shutdown. This applies even if a successful restart is accomplished. Exception: Intentional shutdowns for Functional Check Flights (FCFs).

7.5. Radio Failure:

7.5.1. General. Individual aircraft experiencing radio failure will comply with procedures outlined in FLIP, AFI 11-205, AFI 11-202V3, this volume, and local directives.

7.5.2. Formation:

7.5.2.1. Flight members who experience total radio failure while in close or route formation will maneuver within close/route parameters to attract the attention of another flight member and give the appropriate visual signals. Consider using a J28.2 text message to make contact with other flight members. Using the survival radio is an option as well. Terminate the mission as soon as practical and lead the NORDO aircraft to the base of intended landing or a divert base. Perform a formation approach to a drop-off on final unless safety, fuel, weather, or other considerations dictate otherwise.

7.5.2.2. If flying other than close/route formation when radio failure occurs, the NORDO aircraft should attempt to rejoin to a route position on another flight member. The joining/wing aircraft is responsible for deconfliction until the other flight member acknowledges his presence by a wing rock, signifying clearance to join. Once joined, the NORDO aircraft will give the appropriate visual signals. If prebriefed, the NORDO aircraft may proceed to a rendezvous point and hold. If no one has rejoined prior to reaching BINGO fuel, the NORDO aircraft should proceed to the base of intended landing or a divert base IAW paragraph **7.5.1** above. Aircraft experiencing any difficulty/emergency in addition to NORDO will proceed as required by the situation.

7.5.3. Surface Attack NORDO Procedures for Class A/Manned Class B Ranges:

7.5.3.1. Attempt contact with the RCO on the appropriate backup frequency.

7.5.3.2. If unable to re-establish contact, make a pass by the range control tower on the attack heading while rocking wings, and turn in the direction of traffic. The flight leader will either rejoin on the NORDO aircraft, or direct another flight member to rejoin on the NORDO aircraft, in order to escort the NORDO aircraft to a recovery base.

7.5.3.3. If the NORDO aircraft has an emergency, make a pass by the range control tower, if practical, on the attack heading while rocking wings, turn opposite the direction of traffic, and proceed to a recovery base. The flight leader will either rejoin on the NORDO aircraft, or direct another flight member to rejoin on the NORDO aircraft, in order to escort the emergency aircraft.

7.5.3.4. If the RCO experiences radio failure, the flight will hold high and maintain spacing while attempting contact on primary and backup frequencies.

7.5.3.5. If radio failure occurs and circumstances preclude landing with unexpended ordnance, safe jettison of ordnance may be accomplished provided the following conditions are met:

7.5.3.5.1. The NORDO aircraft joins on another flight member that has radio contact with the RCO and the remainder of the flight.

7.5.3.5.2. Stores jettison visual signals specified in AFI 11-205 are relayed to the NORDO aircraft to initiate jettison.

7.5.4. Surface Attack NORDO Procedures for Unmanned Class B and Class C Ranges:

7.5.4.1. Make a "high and dry" pass on the target, if possible, while rocking wings.

7.5.4.2. The leader will either rejoin the flight in sequence and recover, or direct another flight member to escort the NORDO aircraft to a recovery base.

7.5.4.3. If the NORDO has an emergency, he will, if practical, make a pass on the target, rocking wings, turn opposite direction of traffic, and proceed to a recovery base. The flight leader will either rejoin on the NORDO aircraft, or direct a flight member to rejoin on the NORDO aircraft, in order to escort the emergency aircraft.

7.5.5. NORDO Recovery:

7.5.5.1. The procedures in AFI 11-205 and FLIP apply.

7.5.5.2. If flying a straight-in approach and a go-around becomes necessary, the chase will go-around, pass the NORDO aircraft and rock his wings.

7.5.5.3. The NORDO aircraft will go-around if the situation allows. If the NORDO aircraft is in formation as a wingman, the leader will initiate a gentle turn into the wingman and begin the go-around.

7.6. Severe Weather Penetration:

7.6.1. Do not attempt flight through severe weather. However, if unavoidable, obtain separate clearances prior to severe weather penetration. If not feasible, flights may assume an in-trail formation with a minimum of 1 NM separation between aircraft/elements. Obtain ATC clearance for a non-standard formation.

7.7. Lost Wingman Procedures. In any lost wingman situation, immediate separation of aircraft is essential. Upon losing sight of the leader or unable to maintain formation due to spatial disorientation (SD), the wingman will simultaneously execute the applicable lost wingman procedures while transitioning to instruments and inform the flight lead. Refer to paragraph **7.8** for specific SD considerations. Smooth application of control inputs is imperative to minimize the effects of SD. Permission from the flight lead is required to rejoin the flight once lost wingman procedures have been executed.

7.7.1. Two- or Three-Ship Flights:

7.7.1.1. Wings-Level Flight. In wings-level flight (climb, descent, or straight and level) simultaneously inform lead and turn away using 15 degrees of bank for 15 seconds, then resume heading and obtain separate clearance.

7.7.1.2. Turns:

7.7.1.2.1. Outside the Turn. Reverse the direction of turn using 15 degrees of bank for 15 seconds and inform lead. Continue straight ahead to ensure separation prior to resuming the turn. Obtain a separate clearance.

7.7.1.2.2. Inside the Turn. Momentarily reduce power to ensure nose-tail separation, and inform the flight lead to roll out of the turn. Maintain angle of bank to ensure lateral separation and obtain separate clearance. Once assured separation, the leader may resume turn.   **Note:** If in three-ship echelon, refer to four-ship lost wingman procedures.

7.7.1.3. Precision/Non-Precision Final. The wingman will momentarily turn away to ensure separation, inform lead, and commence the published missed approach procedure while obtaining a separate clearance from approach control.

7.7.1.4. Missed Approach. The wingman will momentarily turn away to ensure separation, inform lead, and continue the published or assigned missed approach procedure while climbing to 500 feet above missed approach altitude. Obtain a separate clearance from approach control.

7.7.2. Four-Ship Flights. If only one aircraft in the flight becomes separated, the previous procedures will provide safe separation. Since it is impossible for number 4 to immediately ascertain that number 3 still has visual contact with lead, it is imperative that initial action of number 4's be based on the assumption that number 3 has also become separated. Number 2 and 3 will follow the procedures outlined above. Number 4 will follow the appropriate procedure listed below:

7.7.2.1. Wings-Level Flight. Simultaneously inform lead and turn away using 30 degrees of bank for 30 seconds, then resume heading and obtain separate clearance.

7.7.2.2. Turns:

7.7.2.2.1. Outside the Turn. Reverse direction of turn using 30 degrees of bank for 30 seconds to ensure separation from lead and number 3 and obtain separate clearance.

7.7.2.2.2. Inside the Turn. Momentarily reduce power to ensure nose-tail separation and increase bank angle by 15 degrees. Inform lead to roll out. Obtain separate clearance. Lead will resume turn only when separation is ensured.

7.7.3. Flight Lead. The flight lead should acknowledge the lost wingman's radio call and transmit attitude, heading, altitude, airspeed and other parameters as appropriate. Wingman will base lost wingman procedure on the flight lead's transmitted parameters (use caution observing published terrain clearance limits).

7.7.3.1. Flight leads will be directive to ensure aircraft separation as required by the situation.

7.7.4. Wingman. If a wingman becomes separated and any aircraft experiences radio failure, the aircraft with the operational radio will obtain a separate clearance. NORDO aircraft will ensure the appropriate IFF/SIF code is selected IAW either the Flight Information Handbook or national rules while proceeding with the previous clearance. If an emergency situation arises along with radio failure, select IFF/SIF to emergency (7700) for the remainder of the flight.

7.7.5. Practice. Practice lost wingman procedures only in VMC.

7.8. Spatial Disorientation. Conditions which prevent a clear visual horizon or increase pilot tasking are conducive to SD. To prevent SD, the pilot will make a conscious attempt to increase instrument cross-check rate. When SD symptoms are detected, take the following steps until symptoms abate:

7.8.1. Single Ship:

7.8.1.1. Concentrate on flying basic instruments with frequent reference to the attitude indicator. Use heads-down instruments. Defer non-essential cockpit tasks.

7.8.1.2. If symptoms persist, bring aircraft to straight and level flight with reference to the attitude indicator and maintain straight and level flight, terrain permitting, until symptoms abate, (usually 30 to 60 seconds), and conditions permitting.

7.8.1.3. If necessary, declare an emergency and advise ATC.

7.8.1.4. It is possible for SD to proceed to the point where the pilot is unable to see, interpret, or process information from the flight instruments. Aircraft control in such a situation is impossible. A pilot must recognize when physiological/psychological limits have been exceeded and be prepared to abandon the aircraft.

7.8.2. Formation Lead:

7.8.2.1. A flight lead with SD will advise wingmen that lead has SD and will comply with procedures in paragraph **7.8.1** above.

7.8.2.2. If possible, wingmen should confirm attitude and provide verbal feedback to lead.

7.8.2.3. If symptoms persist, terminate the mission and recover the flight by the simplest and safest means possible.

7.8.3. Formation Wingman:

7.8.3.1. Wingman will advise lead when disorientation makes it difficult to maintain position.

7.8.3.2. Lead will advise wingman of aircraft attitude, altitude, heading, and airspeed.

7.8.3.3. If symptoms persist, lead will establish straight and level flight for 30 to 60 seconds, conditions permitting.

7.8.3.4. If the above procedures are not effective, lead should consider passing the lead to the wingman, provided the leader will be able to maintain situation awareness from a chase position. Transfer lead while in straight and level flight. Once assuming the lead, maintain straight and level flight for 60 seconds. If necessary, terminate the tactical mission and recover by the simplest and safest means possible.

7.8.4. Greater Than Two-Ship Formation. Lead should separate the flight into elements to more effectively handle a wingman with persistent SD symptoms. Establish straight and level flight IAW paragraph **4.4** (Formation Breakup). The element with the SD pilot will remain straight and level while the other element separates from the flight.

7.9. Armament System Malfunctions:

7.9.1. Inadvertent Release:

7.9.1.1. Record switch positions at the time of inadvertent release and provide to armament and safety personnel. Record the impact point, if known.

7.9.1.2. Check armament switches safe and do not attempt further release in any mode. Treat remaining stores as hung ordnance and obtain a chase aircraft during RTB, if practical.

7.9.1.3. If remaining stores present a recovery hazard, jettison in a suitable area on a single pass, if practical.

7.9.2. Failure to Release/Hung Ordnance. If ordnance fails to release when all appropriate switches are set, proceed as follows:

7.9.2.1. Live Ordnance. For hung live ordnance or an aircraft malfunction that precludes further live weapons delivery, refer to 1A-10C-34-1-1. The following procedures also apply:

7.9.2.1.1. Note all release and fusing switches, then safe.

7.9.2.1.2. Attempt to jettison store(s) using jettison or alternate delivery mode. Consider attempting to jettison the rack if ordnance is unsecure or unable to determine security.

7.9.2.1.3. If ordnance remains on the aircraft, follow the hung ordnance recovery procedures.

7.9.2.2. Practice/Inert Ordnance:

7.9.2.2.1. Re-check switch positions and make an additional attempt to expend. If no release occurs, select another mode of delivery in an attempt to expend. Re-attempted release of a BDU-33 from a TER-9 should be accomplished from a diving delivery followed by a climbing safe escape maneuver in order to provide positive G-loading to potentially separate the bomb from a malfunctioning TER.

7.9.2.2.2. If the secondary release mode fails, ordnance from other stations/dispensers may be released providing the aircraft will remain within symmetrical load limits.

7.9.2.2.3. If remaining stores present a recovery hazard, jettison in a suitable area on a single pass, if practical.

7.9.2.2.4. If ordnance remains on the aircraft, follow the hung ordnance recovery procedures.

7.9.3. Hang Fire/Misfire—General:

7.9.3.1. A missile that fires but fails to depart the aircraft is a hangfire. If this occurs, the chase pilot should closely observe and safety check the missile.

7.9.3.2. A missile that fails to fire when all appropriate switches were selected is a misfire. If this occurs, safe the Master Arm switch and follow the hung ordnance recovery procedures.

7.9.3.3. T.O. 1A-10C-34-1-1contains hangfire/misfire procedures for specific ordnance types.

7.9.4. Gun Unsafe. Refer to T.O. 1A-10C-34-1-1. The following procedures also apply:

7.9.4.1. If the gun unsafe light is accompanied by any unusual noise/vibration, or any other indication of gun/aircraft damage, the pilot will declare an emergency.

7.9.4.2. Accomplish gear lowering over an unpopulated area.

7.9.5. Recovery with Weapons Malfunction/Hung Ordnance:

7.9.5.1. If practical, visually inspect the aircraft for damage.

7.9.5.2. Declare an emergency (not required for hung practice/inert ordnance or rockets).

7.9.5.3. Obtain a chase aircraft, if available, and avoid populated areas and trail formations.

7.9.5.4. Land from a straight-in approach, or IAW local hung ordnance procedures.

7.9.5.5. In case of a delayed BDU-33 release, write up the incident in the AFTO Forms 781, *ARMS Aircrew/Mission Flight Data Document* and declare the aircraft code-3 during maintenance debrief. A delayed release occurs when the BDU-33 releases from the TER-9/A later than planned by the pilot and impacts more than 300 meters long of the target or hangs and subsequently falls off the aircraft later in the sortie.

7.9.6. Miscellaneous Procedures:

7.9.6.1. Pilots will not attempt to expend ordnance using a delivery system with a known weapons release malfunction.

7.9.6.2. When abnormal missile launch or erratic missile flight is noted after launch, another aircraft will visually inspect the launching aircraft (if possible) to determine if any damage has occurred.

7.10. In-flight Practice of Emergency Procedures:

7.10.1. Simulated Emergency Procedures--Definition. Any procedure that produces an effect that would closely parallel the actual emergency such as retarding the throttle to idle and disengaging the SAS to simulate a single engine situation.

7.10.2. Emergency Practice:

7.10.2.1. Accomplish all practice and/or training related to aborted takeoffs in a Cockpit Familiarization Trainer (CFT), Full Motion Trainer (FMT) or a static aircraft (if trainers unavailable).

7.10.2.2. Practice in-flight engine shutdown is prohibited (except during FCF profiles).

7.10.2.3. While in-flight, simulated loss of both engines is prohibited.

7.10.3. Simulated Single Engine (SSE) Approach/ Landing:

7.10.3.1. Do not initiate simulated single engine failure below 1,000 feet AGL and terminate if the aircraft descends below 800 feet AGL prior to base leg or the airspeed drops below computed final approach speed for the aircraft configuration.

7.10.3.2. Follow procedures in T.O. 1A-10C-1 for emergency landing patterns and actual single engine approaches as appropriate for the simulated engine failure situation. Pilots will engage anti-skid prior to landing.

7.10.3.3. Pilots will plan approaches to avoid turns into the simulated dead engine when practical. If turns into the simulated dead engine are necessary, plan patterns to minimize bank angle.

7.10.3.4. IQT or MQT pilots will not perform simulated single engine full stop landings unless chased by an IP.

7.10.3.5. Simulated single engine approaches not terminating in a full stop landing will utilize both engines during go-around, except single engine training conducted above 5,000 feet AGL.

7.10.4. Practice of emergency landing patterns at active airfields is authorized provided that:

7.10.4.1. Adequate crash rescue and air traffic control facilities are available and in operation.

7.10.4.2. The pilot is CMR/BMC. MQT pilots may practice emergency landing patterns when chased by a qualified flight lead. IQT pilots must be chased by an IP.

7.10.4.3. Radio calls at pattern entry and as directed locally or by the controlling agency include the type emergency being simulated.

7.11. Manual Reversion Approach and Landing. Factors to consider are pilot proficiency, instrument approach facilities, runway conditions, weather at the recovery field, and any accompanying aircraft malfunctions. Controlled bailout is recommended anytime existing conditions may preclude a safe recovery or during single engine operations.

7.11.1. Flying in manual reversion is something that is done infrequently and must be treated accordingly. A thorough review of manual reversion procedures in the Dash-1 and/or Dash-6 will be accomplished before any flights where manual reversion is a mandatory part of the flight profile. Particular attention will be placed on actions to be taken when problems arise with manual reversion flight. The first action must be to revert to the normal flight control mode. If that action does not solve the problem and the aircraft is uncontrollable, then ejection is recommended.

7.11.2. Pilots who fly in manual reversion must be completely aware of the characteristics of, problems associated with, and procedures to use with manual reversion.

7.11.2.1. Other than actual emergencies requiring manual reversion, pilots will only go into manual reversion when on a dedicated FCF, FCF upgrade sortie or FTU upgrade sortie.

7.11.2.2. Aircraft must have less than 350 rounds of 30 mm and a configuration of symmetrically loaded TERS, empty TERS, rocket pods or clean to use manual reversion.

7.11.2.3. If aircraft will not go into Manual Reversion or the pitch trim does not work, return Manual Reversion switch to NORM.

7.12. Search and Rescue (SARCAP) Procedures. In the event an aircraft is lost in flight, actions must begin to locate possible survivors and initiate rescue efforts. It is critical all flight members aggressively pursue location and rescue of downed personnel even though they seem uninjured. Many downed aircrews initially suffer from shock or have delayed reactions to ejection injuries. The following procedures are by no means complete and may require adjustment to meet each unique search and rescue situation. **Chapter 8**, Local Operating Procedures, **8.2.2.6**, Abnormal Procedures, details specific procedures.

7.12.1. SQUAWK. Immediately terminate maneuvering using appropriate Knock-It-Off procedures. Establish a SARCAP commander. Place IFF to EMER to alert ATC or Ground Control Intercept (GCI) of the emergency situation.

7.12.2. TALK. Communicate the emergency situation and aircraft/flight intentions immediately to control agencies. Use GUARD frequency if necessary.

7.12.3. MARK. Mark the last known position of survivor/crash site using any means available. Use TACAN/INS position, TAD or TGP marks, ATC/GCI positioning, or ground references to identify the immediate area for subsequent rescue efforts.

7.12.4. SEPARATE. Remain above the last observed parachute altitudes until determining the position of all possible survivors. Deconflict other aircraft in the SARCAP by altitude to preclude midair collision. Establish high/low CAPs as necessary to facilitate communications with other agencies.

7.12.5. BINGO. Revise BINGO fuels or recovery bases as required to maintain maximum SARCAP coverage over survivor/crash site. Do not overfly BINGO fuel. Relinquish SARCAP operation to designated rescue forces upon their arrival.

7.13. Chemical, Biological, Radiological, Nuclear and High Yield Explosive (CBRNE) Operations. For CBRNE operations see Attachment 16.

Chapter 8

LOCAL OPERATING PROCEDURES

8.1. General. This chapter is reserved for unit local operating procedures. Units composed of dissimilar aircraft may publish guidance in a single, stand-alone local operating instruction (OI) instead of supplementing this AFI. Added or stand-alone procedures will not be less restrictive than those contained elsewhere in this volume. This chapter is not intended to be a single source document for procedures contained in other directives or regulations. Avoid unnecessary repetition of guidance provided in other established directives; however, reference to those directives is acceptable when it serves to facilitate location of information necessary for local operating procedures. This chapter is authorized to be issued to each A-10 pilot.

8.2. Procedures. Unless changed by MAJCOM or subordinate agency, the following procedures apply:

8.2.1. Organize the local chapter in the following format to include, but not limited to, the following:

8.2.1.1. Section A—Introduction

8.2.1.2. Section B—General Policy

8.2.1.3. Section C—Ground Operations

8.2.1.4. Section D—Flying Operations

8.2.1.5. Section E—Weapons Employment

8.2.1.6. Section F--Abnormal Procedures

8.2.1.7. Attachments (Illustrations)

8.2.2. This chapter will include procedures for the following, if applicable:

8.2.2.1. Command and Control

8.2.2.2. Fuel Requirements and Bingo Fuels

8.2.2.3. Diversion Instructions

8.2.2.4. Jettison Areas (IFR/VFR)

8.2.2.5. Jettison Procedures/Parameters

8.2.2.6. Controlled Bailout Areas

8.2.2.7. Local Weather Procedures

8.2.2.8. Securing Aircraft After Emergencies

8.2.2.9. Approved Alternate Missions

8.2.2.10. Cross-Country/Servicing Procedures

8.2.2.11. Search and Rescue (SARCAP) Procedures

8.3. Distributing Guidance. When published, units will forward copies of local operation procedures to their respective MAJCOMs and appropriate subordinate agencies for review and comment. Distribution of local guidance may begin before the review process is complete unless otherwise specified by MAJCOM or appropriate subordinate agency. If a procedure is deemed applicable to all A-10 units, it will be incorporated into the basis AFI volume.

HERBERT J. CARLISLE, Lt Gen, USAF
DCS, Operations, Plans and Requirements

Attachment 1

GLOSSARY OF REFERENCES AND SUPPORTING INFORMATION

References

AFI 11-2A/OA-10V1, *A/OA-10--Aircrew Training*, 31 Aug 2006

AFI 11-202V3, *General Flight Rules*, 22 Oct 2010

AFI 11-205, *Aircraft Cockpit and Formation Flight Signals*, 19 May 1994

AFI 11-209, *Aerial Event Policy and Procedures*, 4 May 2006

AFI 11-214, *Air Operations Rules and Procedures*, 22 Dec 2005

AFI 11-218, *Aircraft Operations and Movement on the Ground*, 28 Oct 2011

AFI 33-360, *Publications and Forms Management*, 18 May 2006

AFMAN 11-217V1, *Instrument Flight Procedures*, 22 Oct 2010

AFMAN 33-363, *Management of Records*, 01 Mar 2008

AFPD 11-2, *Aircraft Rules and Procedures*, 14 Jan 2005

AFPD 11-4, *Aviation Service*, 1 Sep 2004

AFTTP 3-1.A-10, *Tactical Employment—A-10 (Secret)*, 16 Sep 2011

AFTTP 3-3.A-10, *Combat Aircraft Fundamentals--A-10*, 11 Feb 2010

FLIP, *Flight Information Publication*

TO 1A-10-1, *Flight Manual—A-10*, 10 Sep 2011

TO 1A-10-34-1-1, *A-10C Non-Nuclear Weapon Delivery Manual*, 10 Sep 2011

Adopted Forms

AF Form 847, Recommendation for Change of Publication

AFTO Form 781, ARMS Aircrew/Mission Flight Data Document

Abbreviations and Acronyms

ACBT—Air Combat Training

(D)ACBT—(Dissimilar) Air Combat Training

ACM—Air Combat Maneuvering

AGL—Above Ground Level

AOA—Angle of Attack

APU—Auxiliary Power Unit

ATC—Air Traffic Control

AWACS—Airborne Warning and Control System

AWE—Aircraft, Weapons and Electronics

BFM—Basic Fighter Maneuvers

BIT—Built in test

BMC—Basic Mission Capable

BOC—Bomb on Coordinate

CDU—Central Display Unit

CICU—Central Interface Control Unit

CMR—Combat Mission Ready

CMS—Countermeasure System

CONUS—Continental United States

DACT—Dissimilar Air Combat Tactics

DO—Director of Operations

DSMS—Digital Stores Management System

DTC—Data Transfer Cartridge

DVADR—Digital Video Airborne Data Recorder

EGI—Embedded GPS/INS

ECM—Electronic Countermeasures

EMCON—Emission Control

EOR—End of Runway

FAC(A)—Forward Air Controller (Airborne)

FAF—Final Approach Fix

FCF—Functional Check Flight

FCIF—Flight Crew Information File

FLIP—Flight Publications

FTU—Formal Training Unit

FWS—Fighter Weapons School

GCAS—Ground Collision Avoidance System

GCI—Ground Control Intercept

HMCS—Helmet Mounted Cueing System

HUD—Head Up Display

IAM—Inertially Aided Munition

IDM—Improved Data Modem

IFF—Identification, Friend or Foe

IFR—Instrument Flight Rules

IFFCC—Integrated Flight and Fire Computer

IMC—Instrument Meteorological Conditions

INS—Inertia Navigation System

IQT—Initial Qualification Training

IR—Instrument Route

JOAP—Joint Oil Analysis Program

JTAC—Joint Tactical Air Controller

LASTE—Low Altitude Safety and Targeting Enhancement

MCOPR—MAJCOM Office of Primary Responsibility

MFCD—Multi-Function Color Display

MOA—Military Operating Area

MSA—Minimum Safe Altitude

MSL—Mean Sea Level

MTR—Military Training Route

MVR—Maneuver

MWS—Missile Warning System

NGB—National Guard Bureau

NORDO—No Radio

NVG—Night Vision Goggles

NVIS—Night Vision Imaging System

PDM—Programmed Delivery for Maintenance

PGCAS—Predictive Ground Collision Avoidance System

PNVG—Panoramic Night Vision Goggles

PWC—Pilot Weather Category

RCO—Range Control Officer

RCR—Runway Conditions Reading

RMMD—Removable Mass Memory Device

ROE—Rule of Engagement

RWR—Radar Warning Receiver

SA—Surface Attack or Situational Awareness

SADL—Situational Awareness Data Link

SAT—Surface Attack Tactics

SIF—Selective Identification

SQ—Squadron

SUA—Special Use Airspace

TACAN—Tactical Air Navigation

TAD—Tactical Awareness Display

TGP—Targeting Pod

TOLD—Take off Landing Data

TOT—Time over Target

TTT—Time to Target

VFR—Visual Flight Rules

VLD—Visual Level Delivery

VMC—Visual Meteorological Conditions

VMF—Variable Message Format

VR—Visual Route

Attachment 2

GENERAL BRIEFING GUIDE

A2.1. Mission Preparation:

A2.1.1. Time Hack

A2.1.2. EP/Threat of the Day

A2.1.3. Mission Objective(s)

A2.1.4. Mission Overview

A2.1.5. Mission Data Card

A2.1.5.1. Mission Commander/Deputy Lead

A2.1.5.2. Joker/Bingo Fuel

A2.1.5.3. Takeoff and Landing Data

A2.1.5.4. Working Area

A2.1.6. Environmental Conditions

A2.1.6.1. Weather/TDA

A2.1.6.2. Sunrise/Sunset (If Applicable)

A2.1.6.3. Moon Illumination (If Applicable)

A2.1.7. NOTAMs

A2.1.8. Personal Equipment

A2.1.9. FCIF/Pubs/Maps

A2.2. Ground Procedures:

A2.2.1. Pre-Flight

A2.2.1.1. Aircraft

A2.2.1.2. Armament

A2.2.2. Ground Crew Briefing (When Applicable)

A2.2.2.1. Act only on Pilot's instructions

A2.2.2.2. Ground emergency procedures

A2.2.2.3. Hand signals

A2.2.2.4. Aircraft Danger Areas

A2.2.3. Check-in

A2.2.4. Taxi/Marshalling/Arming

A2.2.5. Spare Procedures

A2.3. Takeoff:

A2.3.1. Runway Lineup

A2.3.2. Formation Takeoff

A2.3.3. Takeoff Interval

A2.3.4. Abort

A2.3.5. Landing Immediately After Takeoff

A2.4. Departure:

A2.4.1. Routing

A2.4.2. Trail Departure

A2.4.3. Rejoin

A2.4.4. Formation

A2.4.5. Ops Checks

A2.5. Recovery:

A2.5.1. Rejoin

A2.5.2. Battle Damage/Bomb Check (If Applicable)

A2.5.3. Flight Breakup (If Applicable)

A2.5.4. Contingency Routing

A2.5.4.1. Hung/Unexpended Ordnance (If Applicable)

A2.5.4.2. Weapons/Aircraft Malfunction (If Applicable)

A2.5.5. Pattern and Landing

A2.5.6. Landing/De-Arm

A2.5.7. Emergency / Alternate Airfields

Attachment 3

SPECIAL SUBJECTS BRIEFING GUIDE

A3.1. General Roles and Responsibilities (IP, Flight Lead, Wingman).

A3.1.1. Formation Specific Responsibilities and Priorities

A3.1.2. Flight Member Mission Priorities

A3.1.3. Sensor Prioritization

A3.1.4. Deconfliction Contracts

A3.1.5. Instructor Responsibilities

A3.2. Chase Procedures

A3.3. IFF Procedures

A3.4. Visual Search Responsibilities/Midair Collision Avoidance/Flight Path Deconfliction

A3.4.1. Departure/Enroute/Recovery

A3.4.2. High Density Traffic Areas

A3.4.3. From Other Military Aircraft

A3.4.4. From Civilian Aircraft

A3.5. Dissimilar Formations.

A3.6. Terrain Avoidance:

A3.6.1. Departure/En Route/Recovery

A3.6.2. Use of Radar Altimeters / GCAS

A3.6.3. Ejection decision (i.e., immediately after T/O, prior to landing, departing a prepared surface, high altitude, low altitude)

A3.7. Bird Strike Procedures.

A3.8. Hazards Associated With Human Factors (i. e., Channelized Attention, Task Saturation/Prioritization, and Complacency).

A3.9. G-Awareness:

A3.9.1. Turn/G-Suit Connection/G-tolerance

A3.9.2. Use of L-1 Anti-G Straining Maneuver (AGSM)

A3.10. Visual Illusions/Perceptions.

A3.11. Spatial Disorientation/Unusual Attitudes/G-Excess Illusion.

A3.12. Lost Wingman.

A3.13. Radio Inoperative.

A3.14. SARCAP.

A3.15. Recall Procedures.

A3.16. SIIs.

A3.17. Training Rules / Special Operating Instructions.

Attachment 4

INSTRUMENT/NAVIGATION BRIEFING GUIDE

A4.1. Climb:

A4.1.1. Instrument Departure

A4.1.1.1. Power Setting/Airspeed

A4.1.1.2. Trail Departure (If Applicable)

A4.1.1.3. Routing (SID, Radar Vectors, etc.)

A4.1.2. Level Off

A4.1.3. Formation

A4.2. Cruise:

A4.2.1. En route

A4.2.2. Cruise Data

A4.2.3. Nav Aids

A4.2.4. Fuel Awareness/Ops Checks

A4.3. Area:

A4.3.1. Airwork

A4.3.1.1. Airspace Restrictions

A4.3.1.2. Area Orientation

A4.3.1.3. Instructor Responsibilities (If Applicable)

A4.3.1.4. Maneuvers/G-Awareness

A4.4. Approaches:

A4.4.1. Frequencies

A4.4.2. Holding

A4.4.3. Penetration

A4.4.4. Missed Approach/Climb out

A4.5. Special Subjects:

A4.5.1. Alternate Mission

A4.5.2. Emergency/Alternate Airfields

A4.5.3. Spatial Disorientation

A4.5.4. Unusual Attitudes

A4.5.5. Hazards Associated With Human Factors (i.e., Channelized Attention, Task Saturation/Prioritization, and Complacency)

Attachment 5

AIR REFUELING BRIEFING GUIDE

A5.1. General:

A5.1.1. Tanker Call Sign(s), Receiver Assignments

A5.1.2. Refueling Track(s), (Altitude and airspeed)

A5.1.3. Radio Frequencies

A5.1.4. ARIPs, ARCPs, ARCTs

A5.2. Buddy Procedures:

A5.2.1. Departure

A5.2.2. Join-up

A5.3. Enroute:

A5.3.1. Route of Flight

A5.3.2. Formation

A5.3.3. Ops Checks

A5.4. Rendezvous:

A5.4.1. Type Rendezvous

A5.4.2. Holding Procedures/Formation

A5.4.3. Ground Radar Assistance

A5.4.4. Tanker Identification—A/A TACAN/ Ground Radar/ADF/Visual

A5.4.5. Wingman/Deputy Lead Responsibilities

A5.4.6. Receiver Formation/Join-up Procedures

A5.4.7. Rendezvous Overrun

A5.5. Refueling:

A5.5.1. Checklist Procedures

A5.5.2. Radio Calls

A5.5.3. Refueling Order

A5.5.4. Techniques

A5.5.5. Radio Silent Procedures (EMCON/Visual Signals)

A5.5.6. Fuel Off-Load

A5.5.7. Abort Points/Abort Bases

A5.5.8. Drop-Off Procedures

A5.5.9. Wake Turbulence

A5.6. Rejoin and Exit:

A5.6.1. Formation

A5.6.2. Clearance

A5.7. Emergency Procedures:

A5.7.1. Breakaway Procedures

A5.7.2. Systems Malfunctions

A5.7.3. Damaged Receptacle

A5.8. IMC/Night Considerations (If Applicable):

A5.8.1. Lost Wingman Procedures

A5.8.1.1. Enroute

A5.8.1.2. On the Tanker

A5.8.2. Aircraft Lighting

A5.9. Special Subjects:

A5.9.1. Alternate Mission

A5.9.2. Spatial Disorientation

A5.9.3. Hazards Associated with Human Factors (i.e., Channelized Attention, Task Saturation/Prioritization, and Complacency)

Attachment 6

(D) ACBT BRIEFING GUIDE

A6.1. General:

A6.1.1. Call Signs

A6.1.2. Number and Type Aircraft

A6.1.3. Dissimilar Formation (If Applicable)

A6.1.3.1. Formation References

A6.1.3.2. In-flight Visual Signals

A6.1.4. Debriefing (Time/Place)

A6.1.5. G-Awareness/Tolerance/Warm-up

A6.1.6. Area Information

A6.1.6.1. Controlling Agency

A6.1.6.2. Airspace Limits/Restrictions

A6.1.6.3. Frequencies

A6.1.6.4. Squawks

A6.1.6.5. Block Altitudes/Minimum Altitudes

A6.2. Tactical:

A6.2.1. Scenario

A6.2.1.1. Type Threat Simulated/Tactics Limitations

A6.2.1.2. Safe Areas/FEBA

A6.2.1.3. Ingress/Egress Routing/Target Locations

A6.2.2. LOWAT (If Applicable)

A6.2.2.1. Minimum Altitudes

A6.2.2.2. Maneuvering Limitations

A6.2.3. BFM

A6.2.3.1. Setups

A6.2.3.2. Offensive

A6.2.3.3. Defensive

A6.2.4. Flight/Element Tactics

A6.2.4.1. Tactics/Mutual Support

A6.2.4.2. Formation /Look out Responsibilities

A6.2.4.3. Roles and Responsibilities

A6.2.4.3.1. Engaged

A6.2.4.3.2. Supporting

A6.2.4.4. Clearance for Wingman to Engage

A6.2.4.5. Radio Usage

A6.2.4.6. Egress/Separate/Rejoin

A6.2.4.7. Termination

A6.2.5. Weapons Employment

A6.2.5.1. Weapons System/RWR/ECM/IFF Checks

A6.2.5.2. Simulated Ordnance (Type/Quantity)

A6.2.5.3. Shot Criteria/Air-to-Air Weapons Switchology

A6.2.5.4. Kill Criteria/Removal

A6.3. Specific Mission Considerations:

A6.3.1. Air to Air Training Rules

A6.3.2. Midair Collision Avoidance/Flight Path Deconfliction (With/Without Visual)

A6.3.3. Maneuvering Limitations

A6.3.3.1. AOA/Airspeed and G

A6.3.3.2. Recognition/Prevention/Recovery from Out of Control

A6.3.3.3. Heavy Gross Weight Effect on Maneuvering

A6.3.3.4. Limitations

A6.3.3.4.1. Aircraft

A6.3.3.4.2. Ordnance

A6.3.3.5. Asymmetrical Configuration/Thrust

A6.3.3.6. Adverse Yaw/Accelerated Stalls

A6.3.3.7. Stalls/Departures

A6.3.3.7.1. Engine Stall Susceptibility

A6.3.3.7.2. Flight Control Effectiveness

A6.3.3.7.3. Use of AOA/Aural Tones

A6.3.3.8. A-10 vs A-10 unique considerations

A6.3.3.9. A-10 vs High Speed Fighter

A6.3.3.10. Energy/Thrust Limitations

A6.4. Special Subjects:

A6.4.1. Emergencies/Escort/Dissimilar Formation Recovery (If Applicable)

A6.4.2. Additional Considerations

    A6.4.2.1. Film/VTR

    A6.4.2.2. Tape Recorders

    A6.4.2.3. Air-to-Air TACAN

    A6.4.2.4. Codewords

    A6.4.2.5. Environmental Considerations (Sun angle, etc.)

A6.4.3. Hazards Associated with Human Factors (i.e., Channelized Attention, Task Saturation/Prioritization, and Complacency)

A6.4.4. Alternate Mission

Attachment 7

ESCORT MISSION BRIEFING GUIDE

A7.1. En route To Rendezvous/Post-Mission Navigation:

A7.1.1. Formation

A7.1.2. Route of Flight/Applicable Restrictions

A7.1.3. Control Agency Callsign/Frequency

A7.2. Rendezvous:

A7.2.1. Protected Force Callsign/Common Frequency

A7.2.2. Number/Type Aircraft

A7.2.3. Rendezvous Point/Time

A7.2.4. Altitude

A7.2.5. Airspeed

A7.3. Escort Procedures:

A7.3.1. Type Formation

A7.3.2. Tactics/Mutual Support

A7.3.3. Escort Route/Airspeed

A7.3.4. Weapons Considerations

A7.3.5. ECM/RWR

A7.4. Training Rules.

Attachment 8

LOW LEVEL NAVIGATION/LOW ALTITUDE TACTICAL NAVIGATION (LATN)
BRIEFING GUIDE

A8.1. General:

A8.1.1. Route/Clearance/Restrictions

A8.1.2. Flight Responsibilities

A8.1.2.1. Navigation

A8.1.2.2. Visual Search Responsibilities

A8.1.2.3. Radio Procedures

A8.1.2.4. Entry/Spacing/Holding

A8.2. Route Procedures:

A8.2.1. Airspace Restrictions

A8.2.2. Fence Checks

A8.2.3. Tactical Formation/Turns

A8.2.4. G-Awareness/Warm-up

A8.2.5. Low Level Navigation

A8.2.5.1. Map Preparation/Pilotage/Dead Reckoning

A8.2.5.2. Use of Nav Aids/EGI

A8.2.5.3. Visual Search Techniques

A8.2.5.4. Updates

A8.2.5.5. Time/Fuel Control

A8.2.5.6. Use of Terrain/Wingman Considerations

A8.2.5.7. Leg Altitudes/Obstacles (MSL/AGL)

A8.2.5.8. Turn Point Acquisition

A8.2.6. Threat Reactions

A8.2.6.1. CMS Employment/Restrictions

A8.2.6.2. Engagement Criteria

A8.2.6.3. LOWAT (If Applicable)

A8.2.6.4. Flight Path Deconfliction (With/Without Visual)

A8.3. Special Subjects:

A8.3.1. Fuel Awareness/Ops Checks

A8.3.2. Two/Three Ship Options

A8.3.3. Low Level Safety Procedures

A8.3.3.1. Terrain Avoidance

A8.3.3.1.1. AGL/MSL Altitude Alerts

A8.3.3.2. Time to Ground Impact

A8.3.3.2.1. Wings Level

A8.3.3.2.2. Over Bank/Under G

A8.3.3.3. Aircraft and Flight Maneuvering Parameters

A8.3.3.4. Knock-It-Off Criteria/Response

A8.3.3.5. Low Level Emergencies/Malfunctions

A8.3.3.6. Route Abort Procedures (RAA)

A8.3.3.7. Hazards Associated with Human Factors (i.e., Channelized Attention, Task Saturation/Prioritization, and Complacency)

A8.3.3.8. Task Saturation/Prioritization

A8.3.3.9. Visual Illusions/Perceptions

A8.3.4. Alternate Mission/Routing

A8.3.5. Emergency/Alternate Airfields

A8.3.6. Special Operating Instructions (If Applicable)

A8.4. Weapons Employment. Refer to Appropriate Air-to-Surface Employment Briefing Guide.

Attachment 9

AIR-TO-SURFACE WEAPONS EMPLOYMENT RANGE MISSION BRIEFING GUIDE

A9.1. En route—G-Awareness/Warm-up.

A9.2. Range Information:

A9.2.1. Target/Range Description

A9.2.2. Restrictions

A9.2.3. Range Entry/Holding

A9.2.4. Radio Procedures

A9.2.5. Formation

A9.2.6. Sequence of Events

A9.2.7. Pattern Procedures

A9.3. Employment Procedures/Techniques:

A9.3.1. Switch Positions

A9.3.1.1. Arming

A9.3.1.2. Displays

A9.3.1.3. Use of EGI/HUD/LASTE

A9.3.2. Pop-up Delivery

A9.3.2.1. Entry Airspeed/Altitude

A9.3.2.2. Pop Point/Pull-up Angle/Power Setting

A9.3.2.3. Target Acquisition

A9.3.2.4. Pull Down/Apex Altitudes

A9.3.2.5. Pattern Corrections

A9.3.3. Roll-In

A9.3.3.1. Position

A9.3.3.2. Techniques (Pitch/Bank/Power)

A9.3.3.3. Roll-out/Wind Effect

A9.3.4. Final

A9.3.4.1. Aim-Off Distance/IPP

A9.3.4.2. Dive Angle

A9.3.4.3. Airspeed

A9.3.4.4. HUD Depiction

A9.3.4.5. Sight Picture/Corrections/Aim-Point

A9.3.4.6. Release Parameters

A9.3.4.7. Release Indications

A9.3.4.8. Recovery Procedures

A9.4. Night Procedures (If Applicable):

A9.4.1. Aircraft Lighting

A9.4.2. Radio Calls

A9.4.3. Target ID/Range Lighting

A9.4.4. Night Spacing Techniques

A9.4.5. Instrument Cross-check/Disorientation

A9.4.6. Flare Pattern

A9.4.6.1. Flare Release Points and Interval

A9.4.6.2. Wind Effect/Offset

A9.4.6.3. Dud Flare Procedures

A9.4.6.4. Switching Aircraft Patterns

A9.5. Over Water Range Operations:

A9.5.1. Employment Techniques

A9.5.1.1. Depth Perception/Reduced Visual Cues

A9.5.1.2. Distance/Altitude Estimation

A9.5.1.3. Pop-Up Positioning

A9.5.1.3.1. Timing

A9.5.1.3.2. Visual/Aircraft References to Establish Pull-up Point

A9.5.2. Special Considerations

A9.5.2.1. Adjusted Minimum Altitudes

A9.5.2.2. Training Rules/Special Operating Procedures

A9.6. Range Departure/Recovery:

A9.6.1. Armament Safety Checks

A9.6.2. Rejoin

A9.6.3. Battle Damage/Bomb Check

A9.6.4. Hung Ordnance

A9.6.5. Inadvertent/Unintentional Release

A9.6.6. Gun Unsafe/Jam

A9.7. Special Subjects:

Attachment 10

AIR-TO-SURFACE WEAPONS EMPLOYMENT SURFACE ATTACK TACTICS BRIEFING GUIDE

A10.1. General Mission Data:

A10.1.1. Intelligence/Threat Scenario

A10.1.2. Low Level (See Low Level Briefing Guide)

A10.1.3. Fence Checks

A10.1.4. G-Awareness/Warm-up

A10.1.5. Operating Area Entry/Description/ Boundaries

A10.1.6. Target Area/Clearing Pass

A10.1.6.1. Location/Description/Elevation/TOT

A10.1.6.2. Visual Cues in the Target Area

A10.1.6.3. Target Area Weather

A10.1.6.3.1. Ceiling/Visibility

A10.1.6.3.2. Winds/Altimeter

A10.1.6.3.3. Sun Angle/Shadows

A10.1.7. Threat Array

A10.1.7.1. Type/Capabilities

A10.1.7.2. Locations

A10.1.7.3. Countermeasures

A10.1.7.3.1. Chaff/Flare

A10.1.7.3.2. Terrain Masking

A10.1.7.3.3. Radio Silent Procedures

A10.1.7.3.4. Authentication/Comm-Jamming/Chattermark Procedures

A10.1.7.4. Threat Reactions

A10.1.7.4.1. LOWAT (If Applicable)

A10.2. Delivery:

A10.2.1. Tactics

A10.2.1.1. Overview

A10.2.1.2. Ingress

A10.2.1.2.1. Formation

A10.2.1.2.2. Speed/Altitude

A10.2.1.3. Weapons Delivery

A10.2.1.3.1. Type Delivery

A10.2.1.3.2. Switchology

A10.2.1.3.3. Attack Parameters

A10.2.1.3.3.1. Action Point/Pop Point

A10.2.1.3.3.2. Altitudes (Pull-Down/Apex/Release/Minimum)

A10.2.1.3.4. Visual Lookout/Mutual Support Responsibilities

A10.2.1.4. Egress

A10.2.1.4.1. Recovery/Return to Low Altitude

A10.2.1.4.2. Loss of Mutual Support/Rendezvous Point

A10.3. Night Procedures (If Applicable):

A10.3.1. Aircraft Lighting

A10.3.2. Radio Calls

A10.3.3. Target ID/Range Lighting

A10.3.4. Night Spacing Techniques/Minimum Altitudes

A10.3.5. Instrument Cross-check/Disorientation

A10.3.6. Flare Pattern

A10.3.6.1. Flare Release Points and Interval

A10.3.6.2. Wind Effect/Offset

A10.3.6.3. Dud Flare Procedures

A10.3.6.4. Switching Aircraft Patterns

A10.3.7. Rejoin/Range Departure

A10.3.8. Battle Damage/Bomb Check

A10.3.9. Mission Reporting (BDA/In-flight Report)

A10.4. Contingencies:

A10.4.1. Two/Three Ship Options

A10.4.2. Tactical Lead Changes

A10.4.3. Air-to-Air TACAN

A10.4.4. Codewords

A10.4.5. Weather Backup Deliveries

A10.4.6. Degraded Systems

A10.4.7. Reattack

A10.4.8. Asymmetric Considerations

A10.4.9. Jettison Procedures/Parameters

A10.4.10. Hung/Unexpended Ordnance Procedures

A10.4.11. Wounded Bird/Escort Procedures

A10.5. Special Subjects:

A10.5.1. Air-to-Surface Training Rules/Special Operating Instructions

A10.5.2. LOWAT Training Rules (If Applicable)

A10.5.3. Maritime Training Rules (If Applicable)

A10.5.4. Night Procedures (If Applicable)

A10.5.5. Hazards Associated with Human Factors (i.e., Channelized Attention, Task Saturation/ Prioritization, and Complacency)

A10.5.6. Alternate Mission

Attachment 11

**AIR-TO-SURFACE WEAPONS EMPLOYMENT CLOSE AIR
SUPPORT/INTERDICTION/ARMED RECCE FAC/JAAT BRIEFING GUIDE**

A11.1. General Information:

A11.1.1. Intelligence/Threat Scenario

A11.1.2. Low Level (See Low Level Briefing Guide)

A11.1.3. Ordnance/Weapons Data

A11.1.3.1. Type/Fuzing

A11.1.3.2. Weapon Settings

A11.1.3.3. Live Ordnance Procedures/Minimum Altitudes

A11.1.3.3.1. Safe Escape/Safe Separation

A11.1.3.3.2. Fuse Arming/Frag Avoidance

A11.1.3.4. Laser Operations

A11.1.4. En route Formation(s)/Look Out Responsibilities/LOWAT (If Applicable)

A11.1.5. Fence Checks

A11.1.6. G-Awareness/Warm-up

A11.1.7. Control Agency

A11.1.7.1. Call Sign

A11.1.7.2. Frequencies

A11.2. Armed Recce Procedures:

A11.2.1. Recce Route/Altitudes

A11.2.2. Formations

A11.2.3. Target Types

A11.2.4. Engagement Criteria

A11.2.5. Attack Tactics--Refer to Weapons Delivery

A11.3. JAAT Procedures:

A11.3.1. Controlling Agencies

A11.3.1.1. Air Battle Captain (ABC)

A11.3.1.2. HeloFAC

A11.3.2. Coordination

A11.3.2.1. AVN CDR/HeloFAC-to-Fighter Brief

A11.3.2.2. Unmask Call/Code Words

A11.3.2.3. Airspace Restrictions

A11.3.2.3.1. Helicopter Altitude Block

A11.3.2.3.2. Fighter Altitude Block

A11.3.2.3.3. Artillery Corridor/Separation

A11.4. FAC Procedures:

A11.4.1. Call Sign/Mission Number

A11.4.2. Primary/Alternate Target Area

A11.4.2.1. Description

A11.4.2.2. Frequencies

A11.4.3. Rendezvous Point/TOT/Authentication Procedures

A11.4.4. Fighter--FAC Briefing

A11.4.4.1. Mission Number

A11.4.4.2. Ordnance (Simulated/Actual)

A11.4.4.3. Playtime

A11.4.5. FAC--Fighter Briefing

A11.4.5.1. Friendly Position

A11.4.5.2. Restrictions

A11.4.6. Target Description

A11.4.6.1. Location/Elevation

A11.4.6.2. Highest Obstacle within 5 NM

A11.4.6.3. Description

A11.4.6.4. Positions of Enemy/Friendly Troops

A11.4.7. Attack Tactics

A11.4.7.1. Type Attack/Attack Restrictions

A11.4.7.2. Direction of Attack Recovery

A11.4.7.3. Ordnance Delivery Procedures (Refer to Weapons Delivery)

A11.5. Weapons Delivery:

A11.5.1. Tactics

A11.5.1.1. Type Delivery

A11.5.1.2. Switchology

A11.5.1.3. Attack Parameters

A11.5.1.3.1. Action Point/Pop Point

Attachment 12

AIR-TO-SURFACE WEAPONS EMPLOYMENT COMBAT CSAR BRIEFING GUIDE

A12.1. Combat SAR Procedures:

A12.1.1. Enroute to SAR Area

A12.1.1.1. Formation

A12.1.1.2. Route

A12.1.1.3. Cruise Data

A12.1.1.4. Control Agency(s) Call Sign/Frequencies

A12.1.1.5. Holding Points And Procedures

A12.1.1.6. Safe Areas

A12.1.2. Electronic/Visual Search

A12.1.2.1. Minimum Altitudes/Airspeeds

A12.1.2.2. Patterns and Wingman Position/Responsibilities

A12.1.2.3. Radio Procedures

A12.1.2.4. Look-Out Doctrine

A12.1.2.5. Low Altitude Hazards

A12.1.2.6. IP Selection and Ingress Route

A12.1.2.7. Survivor Briefing/Authentication

A12.1.3. Helicopter Rendezvous/Escort

A12.1.3.1. Helicopter Call Sign

A12.1.3.2. Altitude/Airspeed

A12.1.3.3. Helicopter Briefing

A12.1.3.4. Type Formation/Patterns for Escort

A12.1.3.5. Tactics

A12.1.3.6. ECM/RWR

A12.1.3.7. Suppression

A12.1.3.8. Pick-Up Techniques

A12.1.3.9. Hover Cover Patterns

A12.1.3.10. Egress Route/Altitude

A12.1.4. Air Strike Control (ASC) & Strike Coordination and Reconnaissance (SCAR) Procedures

A12.1.5. Ordnance Considerations (Refer to Weapons Delivery)

A12.1.6. Ops Checks

A12.1.7. Fuel Considerations (Tanker Availability)

A12.1.8. After Pick-up Procedures

A12.1.8.1. Target Area Egress, Rejoin, Ordnance Checks and Return Navigation

A12.1.8.2. Recovery with Weapons Malfunctions.

Attachment 13

AIR-TO-SURFACE WEAPONS EMPLOYMENT AIR STRIKE CONTROL BRIEFING GUIDE

A13.1. Intelligence:

A13.1.1. Controlling Agencies

A13.1.2. Enemy Positions/Defenses

A13.1.3. Friendly Positions

A13.1.3.1. Call Sign/Ground Commander/JTAC

A13.1.3.2. Frequencies

A13.1.3.3. Minimum Altitudes

A13.1.4. Threat Information

A13.1.5. E&E/SAFE Areas

A13.1.6. SAR

A13.1.7. Authentication/Code Words

A13.2. Local Operating Procedures.

A13.3. Range/MOA Data:

A13.3.1. Frequencies

A13.3.2. Boundaries

A13.3.3. Entry/Exit

A13.3.4. Restrictions

A13.3.5. G-Awareness/Warm-up

A13.4. FAC Strike Data:

A13.4.1. Fighters/ATO Information

A13.4.1.1. Call Sign/Mission Number/Frequencies

A13.4.1.2. Type Ordnance

A13.4.1.3. Contact Point/TOT

A13.4.1.4. Restrictions

A13.4.2. Sequence of Delivery/Fuzing

A13.4.3. FAC Tactics

A13.4.3.1. Alternate Plan for Weather

A13.4.3.2. Late/No Fighters

A13.4.3.3. Worsening Ground Situation

Attachment 14

NVG CONSIDERATIONS

A14.1. General. Note.   This guide is meant to highlight general NVG considerations, and provides a reference for a basic NVG briefing. All applicable NVG considerations should be incorporated into the specific briefing for the mission being flown.

A14.2. Weather/Illumination:

A14.2.1. Civil/nautical twilight

A14.2.2. Moon rise/set times/phase/elevation/azimuth

A14.2.3. Ceiling/visibility

A14.2.4. LUX/EO TDA

A14.2.5. Obscurants to visibility

A14.3. NVG Preflight:

A14.3.1. Check adjustments/helmet fit and security

A14.3.2. Batteries

A14.3.3. Resolution/focus (eye lane)

A14.3.4. NVG compatible flashlight

A14.4. Cockpit Preflight:

A14.4.1. Cockpit setup

A14.4.2. Cockpit lighting (leaks)/mirrors up

A14.4.3. Cockpit FAM

A14.4.4. Check focus, stow for taxi

A14.5. Before Takeoff:

A14.5.1. Don NVGs/check and adjust/disconnect

A14.5.2. Stow for takeoff

A14.6. Airborne:

A14.6.1. Exterior lights

A14.6.2. Scan pattern

A14.6.2.1. Forward scan

A14.6.2.2. Narrow field of view

A14.6.2.3. Peripheral vision

A14.6.2.4. Scan techniques

A14.6.3. Join-up and enroute altitude/airspeed

A14.6.3.1. Rejoin/closure

A14.6.3.2. Air-Air TACAN

A14.7. Mission:

A14.7.1. Route study/scene interpretation

A14.7.1.1. NVG predictions/ALBIDO

A14.7.1.2. Terrain/shadowing/visual illusions

A14.7.1.3. City/cultural lighting

A14.7.1.3.1. Direction/orientation of lighting

A14.7.2. Aggressive formation maneuvering

A14.7.3. Radar altimeter usage

A14.7.4. Map reading

A14.8. Target Area:

A14.8.1. RV/Holding procedures (NVG differences)

A14.8.2. Target study/acquisition (NVG predictions)

A14.8.3. Deliveries/Pattern procedures

A14.8.3.1. Minimum altitudes

A14.8.3.2. Flight member responsibilities

A14.8.3.3. Moth effect/Deconfliction

A14.8.4. Laser/IR Pointer Operations

A14.8.5. Threat I.D and reaction

A14.8.6. Egress

A14.9. NVG Safety:

A14.9.1. Lost sight--NVGs

A14.9.2. Lost wingman--NVGs

A14.9.3. Depth perception

A14.9.4. Visual illusions

A14.9.5. NVG failure

A14.9.6. Battery failure

A14.9.7. Overconfidence in NVG Capabilities

A14.9.8. Transition to Instruments

A14.9.9. Correct lighting of primary/secondary flight instruments

A14.9.10. Disorientation/misorientation/vertigo

A14.9.11. Target fixation

A14.9.12. Lack of dive information

A14.9.13. Fatigue

A14.9.14. Aircraft emergency

A14.9.15. Ejection--GOGGLES--OFF

Attachment 15

MISSION DEBRIEFING GUIDE

A15.1. Ground Procedures.

A15.2. Takeoff, Join-up, Departure.

A15.3. En route Procedures.

A15.4. Mission Accomplishment/Analysis:

    A15.4.1. Mission Reconstruction

    A15.4.2. Mission Support (FAC, GCI, Helicopters, etc.)

    A15.4.3. VTR/Film Assessment (If Applicable)

    A15.4.4. Learning Objectives Achieved

    A15.4.5. Lessons Learned

    A15.4.6. Anti-G Straining Maneuver Effectiveness

    A15.4.7. Recommendations for Improvement

A15.5. Recovery/Landing/After Landing.

A15.6. General.

    A15.6.1. Radio Procedures

    A15.6.2. Flight Discipline/Effectiveness

    A15.6.3. General Areas for Improvement

A15.7. Comments/Questions.

Attachment 16

CBRNE OPERATIONS

A16.1. General Information. Potential adversary use of CBRNE weapons against a friendly airfield presents a serious threat to flying operations. Although the most effective way for aircrews to avoid this threat is to be airborne before those weapons are detonated/dispersed and then land at a field that has not been contaminated, all personnel must be prepared to operate from a field that has come under CBRNE attack.

A16.2. Mission Preparation. Be aware of the status of the CBRNE environment at the planned launch and recovery airfields, potential divert bases, and throughout the area in which the sortie may fly. Know the current and forecast surface wind direction and the MOPP level in effect for relevant sectors of the airfield. Don appropriate aircrew chemical defense equipment (ACDE) or Ground Crew Ensemble (GCE) to match the appropriate MOPP level (reference AFMAN 10-2602) and carry individual protective equipment (IPE) as required.

A16.3. Stepping to Fly and Aircraft Preflight. This may entail donning ACDE or transitioning from GCE to ACDE. Take precautions to protect aircrew from injury and or contamination while in transit from the squadron facility to the aircraft. If possible, transport aircrew in a vehicle that provides overhead cover (enclosed vehicle). If aircrew travel on foot is unavoidable, choose a route that takes maximum advantage of available overhead cover (sun shades, buildings, etc.) to avoid agents that may be settling from the air. If extra aircrew members are available for preflight duties, consider assigning them to do so wearing GCE. This will allow the aircrew actually flying to minimize exposure.

A16.3.1. Alarm Red (or Theater Equivalent) Prior to Engine Start. If Alarm Red occurs during the step or preflight process, take cover and don appropriate MOPP. This may require use of the ground crew mask. A hardened aircraft shelter (HAS) provides optimum protection, if available. Use caution if entering a HAS that contains aircraft and/or equipment. Close doors after entry. If a HAS or other overhead cover is not immediately available, accept the best rapidly reachable cover.

A16.4. Engine Start to Takeoff. If a HAS is available, use it to minimize exposure time by accomplishing aircraft arming and End of Runway (EOR) procedures inside it (if local procedures permit) and by delaying taxi time as long as possible prior to takeoff.

A16.4.1. Aircraft Launch to Survive (LTS). Units will develop local procedures to provide this option to the commander. In general, aircraft may LTS any time after engine start if they have sufficient fuel and safe, expeditious access to a runway. This option may only be practical for aircraft that are near EOR prior to takeoff or that have just landed.

A16.4.2. Alarm Red Prior to Taxi. If in a HAS, the normal procedure is to shut down. Engine noise may preclude effectiveness of normal alert notification procedures, so ensure ground personnel are aware of the alarm warning, assume proper MOPP, and close HAS doors. Use hand signals if necessary.

A16.4.3. Alarm Red (or Theater Equivalent) After Taxi. Units typically establish procedures for this contingency depending on whether additional protection is available along the taxi route (empty HAS, for instance). Ideally, ground crew sheltering in such a HAS would be available to assist in normal engine shutdown procedures and to close HAS doors. If protection is not available, the best option may be LTS. Maintain contact with Command and Control (C2) entities (Wing Operations Center, Maintenance Operations Center, Supervisor of Flying, etc.) to ensure unity of effort in the overall plan.

A16.5. Takeoff to Landing.

A16.5.1. Contamination. If Chemical Warfare (CW) agent contamination occurred prior to takeoff, flying the aircraft will dissipate the agent to some degree. The total amount of dissipation will be greater with lower flight altitudes and longer flight times. Because the agent may have entered wheel wells, flaps, etc., consider flying in landing configuration to increase airflow to these areas. In any circumstances, merely flying the aircraft is unlikely to achieve complete decontamination.

A16.5.2. Preparing to Land. Aircrew should remain aware of the status of primary and alternate landing locations. Do not attempt to land during Alarm Red situations unless there is no other option. Follow C2 directions and either hold or divert. If mission needs preclude divert, hold until the Alarm Red (or theater equivalent) has cleared or become an Alarm Black. Prior to landing, gain awareness of contaminated sectors of the airfield and of current/forecast surface winds. Use this information in conjunction with C2 direction to plan a route from landing to engine shutdown. The liquid deposition phase following a CW airburst attack can extend up to 1 hour. If landing during Alarm Black, expect a contaminated environment and MOPP 4.

A16.6. Landing to Engine Shutdown. Take advantage of any protection available, minimizing taxi time and distance. Maintain contact with C2 in order to remain aware of unexploded ordnance and/or damage to airfield movement surfaces. If a HAS is available and local procedures permit, accomplish aircraft de-arm and EOR procedures there. If Alarm Red (or Theater Equivalent) occurs between landing and engine shutdown, considerations are similar to those discussed in the engine-start-to-takeoff section.

A16.7. After Engine Shutdown. Don appropriate MOPP if not already worn. If circumstances permit, accomplish normal post-flight inspection procedures. If the aircraft is not contaminated, close the canopy. If there is any suspicion of personnel contamination, aircrew will process through an aircrew contamination control area (ACCA). Accomplish maintenance debriefings under cover to the maximum extent possible.

Attachment 17

WEATHER AND OPERATING MINIMUMS

A17.1. Weather Minimums. Table A17.1 dictates the weather minimums required for several training events.

Table A17.1. Weather Minimum Summary (in feet/nm(km)):

Event	Minimum
Formation Takeoff	300/1nm(1.6km) or PWC*
Formation Landing	500/1.5nm(2.4km) or PWC*
VFR Rejoin	1,500/3nm(5km)
Low Level Navigation	1,500/3nm(5km)
Approach to Field Without DOD Minimums	1,500/3nm(5km)
* Whichever is higher	

A17.2. Minimum Altitudes. Table A17.2 lists the minimum altitudes required for various events and chase positions.

Table A17.2. Minimum Altitude Summary (In Feet):

Event	Minimum
Aerobatics/ACBT/Stalls/Man Reversion	5,000
Change Lead	500 (see note)
Chase (emergency)	300
Chase (IP/SEFE)	50
Formation Low Approaches	100
Low Approaches	Not to touchdown
Knock-It-Off	1,000
Note: 1,000 feet over water; 1,500 feet at night/IMC unless on radar downwind.	

CPSIA information can be obtained
at www.ICGtesting.com
Printed in the USA
LVOW05s2307061017
551545LV00018B/914/P